LEADERS IN ACTION SERIES BOOK ONE

BIBLICAL LEADERSHIP IN TURBULENT TIMES

BASIC PRINCIPLES FOR CHRISTIAN LEADERS

GREGORY E. VON TOBEL

MAHANAIM CREEK PUBLISHERS LLC
WOODINVILLE, WASHINGTON

D1528344

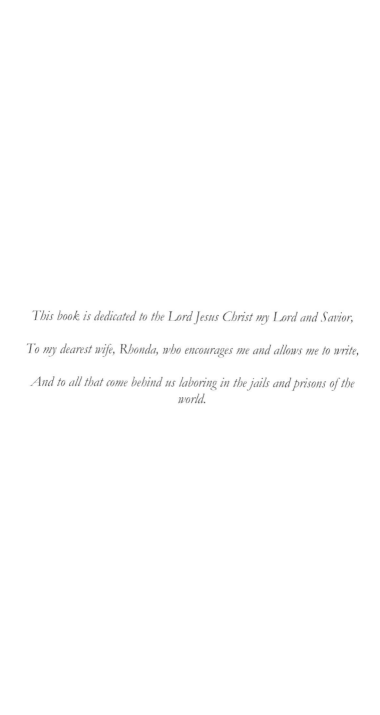

This book is dedicated to the Lord Jesus Christ my Lord and Savior,

To my dearest wife, Rhonda, who encourages me and allows me to write,

And to all that come behind us laboring in the jails and prisons of the world.

CONTENTS

UNIT 1

SPIRITUAL SKILL SET

"Whatever you do, work at it with all your heart, as work-ing for the Lord, not for men, since you know that you will receive an inheritance from the Lord as a reward. It is the Lord Christ you are serving."

Apostle Paul.
Colossians 3:23-24

CHAPTER 1
THE GENESIS

It started out as any other international prison ministry trip. We were four Americans on our way to Rwanda, a new country of expansion, on a mission for Prisoners For Christ (PFC). Rwanda's history—primarily the genocide of 1994 was at the forefront of our minds and in preparation for our trip, we had studied as a team about all that had triggered the genocide. We knew that although over a decade had passed, the people there were still seeing the aftermath of that horrific event in the history of the Rwandan people.

It was through email that we had been invited to come to Rwanda to teach their pastors and lay leaders how to do prison ministry. We had heard that the country (currently under new leadership) was rebounding, and that the Rwandan prison system was now grossly overcrowded with those who had taken part in the genocide. Though we were burdened by the heavy nature of this mission, we embarked on it praying that we would be able to help them in some way.

We are thankful to say that on this trip, we saw PFC's largest prison crusade ever recorded; we had an attendance of over three thousand inmates, with over one thousand inmates who came forward to receive Christ.

As we disembarked from the airplane, we were immediately blasted by the African heat and humidity. And though I had been to Kenya and Uganda several times before and was glad to be back in Africa, I still felt tense as I had never met the people who would be hosting us during our stay in Rwanda. Still, when we arrived, we loaded our luggage into a van and settled in for the hour-long drive it took to get to our hotel. When we arrived, we immediately went into our customary first meeting with our nationals to review and make logistical adjustments, if any, to our twelve-day itinerary.

Naturally, being the time-sensitive, up-tight American that I was, I desired for things to be planned out ahead of time, hopefully even up to the day and hour. I had always struggled with adjusting to last-minute changes on mission trips. This trip was no different.

"Pastor Greg," our host began, "first I want you to know that tomorrow, I have gathered some pastors to meet with you to discuss biblical leadership principles. You will have two hours to teach them."

"But Pastor, that wasn't on the schedule for tomorrow and—" I was about to say I had never preached or shared on leadership principles but decided to keep my thoughts to myself. Although I was now a leader of a small, fledging, regional prison ministry in Washington State, I had never had any formal leadership training apart from reading a couple of leadership books. Back then, finding books on leadership training was similar to finding books on how to be a dad— they were few and far between. I let this conversation slide, wishing that he had asked me to discuss something else, like how to do prison ministry. I could talk about prison ministry all day! But leadership training? I was less enthusiastic.

Still, I looked forward to getting a good night's rest after having endured two long flights. I crept into bed with the plan to jot a few notes down in my Bible in preparation for the next day, but I just couldn't. Jet lag was kicking my rear end and I soon collapsed into a comatose state.

My eyes popped open at 4 a.m., I knew I had to throw something together that would be meaningful to our African brothers. My mind raced as I played roulette with the Bible (that is when you let the pages of the Bible fall open and you quickly skim the pages to see where the Holy Spirit may be leading you.)

My Bible fell open to 1 Corinthians 13, the great *love* chapter. I scanned both of the pages excitedly, but quickly determined that there was nothing on those pages that I could use. I went through this process of Bible roulette several times, but each time I felt the Holy Spirit bringing me back to 1 Corinthians 13. After about five rounds of Bible roulette, I finally went back to 1 Corinthians 13, determined to see what the Holy Spirit wanted me to see.

I felt the Spirit leading me to meditate on the chapter. This came easily as I was already familiar with its principles. I had even endeavored to practice them in my marriage with my dear wife, Rhonda. These principles had made a huge difference in our marriage. The more I had practiced them, the more our marriage grew.

I then had the idea to begin replacing the word *love* with *leadership*; could this passage perhaps be used to build up leaders in Rwanda? I decided that it could and began reading 1 Corinthians 13 in a new light. For the next three hours, I took down copious notes in preparation for the leadership conference. And out of this spur-of-the-moment assignment, came the foundational teaching for our leadership conferences taught around the world today.

As I walked into that Rwandan church midweek, I was expecting maybe a handful of pastors in attendance. Much to my surprise, however, fifty pastors showed up, seated, and ready to listen to what this rookie had to share with them about biblical leadership. Though at first I panicked, as the number of attendees greatly surpassed my expectations, I somehow managed to spend the next two hours delivering to these pastors and lay leaders a message on godly leadership from my notes on 1 Corinthians 13. And much to my surprise, many of these people took down pages and pages of notes. Encouraged by this event, I have added to and honed this message over the years.

CHAPTER 2
IT'S A WONDERFUL LIFE

Today we did something I never thought we would ever do—we shut down the offices of Prisoners For Christ, for at least the next two weeks, which now has turned into eight weeks. Because of the COVID-19 crisis, the prisons and jails in the Pacific Northwest region have all closed their doors to outside visitors. Our governor has shut down all restaurants, movie theatres, and other nonessential businesses in the area. As I watch the world desperately trying to stomp this crisis into oblivion, I am doing my part by penning this book at home, therefore practicing social distancing.

With the fear of the "unknown" on everyone's mind lately, it's evident that the world and the church have never needed godly leaders as much as they do today. It seems as if the world has gone stark raving mad in all avenues of life, with no one to turn to for instructions or even consolation. I never thought I would ever see the day when fear would drive us to run out of toilet paper!

In comparison, when I was a young boy, my mom and dad often talked about life during the Great Depression. They had been just ten and twelve-year-olds when the depression hit, and they remembered it well. I remember them doing their best to explain what it was like for everyone to see a run on the banks—what it was like to live in the fear of the unknown then, too.

A great example of those times is also seen in the movie *It's a Wonderful Life*. My family has a tradition to watch it each year around Christmastime. We have always marveled at the scene where George Bailey and his new wife, Mary, see a panicked bank run occur at their family-owned savings and loan. In the movie, people begin fearing the loss of their savings which leads them to withdraw what they have so they can feed their families.

Seventy-four years after that movie was released, we find ourselves in a similar situation: the masses are making a run on grocery stores to buy toilet paper. This demonstrates two totally opposing world views between the greatest generation that ever lived and those who came after them. This current world view speaks volumes to the priorities of this generation.

Where have all the leaders gone?

I came to know the Lord when I was twenty-seven years old, back when I thought I knew it all when in reality, I actually knew nothing about nothing. It was in these early years of my walk with the Lord that my wife and I began attending a mega church that understood its mandate to evangelize and to disciple. Two days after accepting the Lord as my personal Savior, I received a phone call from some church members who called to invite us to a home fellowship group. We were reluctant, though, as our heads were still swimming at the commitment we had made two days prior. However, the people of this church truly understood the importance of discipleship, and so they upped the ante when they realized we were hesitating. They told us that they would even send someone over to pick us up to take us to this new group. *What? Who does that?*

Because of this extra effort on their part, we accepted their invitation and declined their offer to pick us up since we could drive ourselves to the meeting. I am so glad we went. To this day, we are eternally grateful for this church and the friends we made there who loved on us, discipled us, and taught us the ways of the Lord. For the next ten to twelve years, Rhonda and I learned the principles of the Bible by attending this small group. Had we not become involved with it, I am not quite sure where we would be today.

But where are all these evangelistic Christian leaders today? It seems as if the universal church has moved away from the key church mandates of evangelism and discipleship. The leaders who would stress these mandates are few and far between, causing a blow to new Christians who need to learn the importance of them, just as Rhonda and I did all those years ago. Time has proven that without Christian leaders who are foundationally strong in church doctrine, the church will suffer movements that will blow through, sweeping away these babes in Christ.

I remember on Monday, October 12, 1987, I took my boldest step as a stockbroker. I called all of my clients and advised them to move out of the stock market and sit on the sidelines for the rest of the year. The criticism I received for doing this was overwhelming. Though many believed I was overreacting, about sixty percent of my clients still heeded my advice and saved themselves the stress that came in the following weeks. Black Monday hit us all on October 19, 1987, and the stock market tanked. *A leader leads amid criticisms.* We need more godly leaders in the church today, specifically ones who will disciple those who come behind them.

I remember in the early '90s when the Holy Laughter movement swept through the churches. Where were all the leaders in those churches when that happened? Don't get me wrong, I love a good belly laugh with my friends as much as the next guy does. However, in my opinion, it is irreverent to allow such behavior to continue in a church service when the congregants are there to worship the Lord. There is nowhere in Scripture where this behavior is modeled when worshipping the Lord. Where were the leaders to steer the people in the right direction?

I also remember the Prosperity movement that came through and continues to rear its ugly head in churches. Some say this movement first started in the late fifties in America. However, it really took root with the advent of the bull market that started early in 1990 and the 24-hour TV cycle. How do I know that? I observed it firsthand. This happened during the same time that I left my career as a stockbroker to start Prisoners For Christ. This movement has been incredibly detrimental to the faith walk of many believers around the world. Where were all the good leaders in those churches then?

I remember the Y2K crisis at the turn of the millennium. It instilled fear in the hearts of Christians all over the world. I spoke out against this fearmongering and was promptly chastised by many within the church for not taking it seriously. Still, I stood my ground, firmly declaring that Y2K would not only be but a blip on the radar, but that it would be a nonevent, too. Guess what? Y2K *was* a nonevent and the whole dilemma faded into oblivion, while my reputation became tarnished from the entire episode.

Where were all the leaders then?

CHAPTER 3
THE FROG IN THE KETTLE

In 2016, I published a book called *Staving Off Disaster: A Guide for Christians in Times of Crisis.* It is a book about my journey in spiritual fasting. I wrapped up the book with Chapter 19, "We Are the Generation of the Frog in the Kettle." I have reproduced it below.

> Our country is in trouble! We have a national debt approaching $20 trillion. Our military is being dismantled before our very eyes. The moral underpinnings have all but been eroded. America is the leader in exporting filth and pornography under the auspices of freedom of speech. We have killed more than fifty-five million babies since *Roe v. Wade* in 1973. Our public schools are a disaster. Our Supreme Court judges are making laws, despite the fact that their jobs are to *rule* on laws, not make them.
>
> Our national sovereignty is being whittled away. Jobs are being shipped overseas. Our immigration policies are in shambles. We are now in a national debate on which bathrooms should be used by whom. Everyone is left to their own devices. The millstone noose is quickly tightening around our necks. The people we elect to public offices to be our voices are at loggerheads with one another and are essentially emasculated. Our way of life and our

freedoms are in jeopardy. Down deep we know all of this, but we refuse to take action.

Many of our churches are impotent, producing no fruit. Instead of the Bible shaping our society, society is attempting to shape the Bible. Pastors are leaving the pulpit in droves. Churches were meant to be the launching pads to produce mighty men of God to affect the world for Christ. Instead, they are producing disciples who have no idea on how to take a public stand for what is right.

Many of our Christian Bible colleges are producing students woefully underprepared for the current societal tsunami. Liberalism has slipped into the fold of professors, and tenure is an outdated form of cronyism.

We are that generation—*we are the generation of the frog in the kettle.* We may have crossed the point of no return for the United States of America. Is the hand of God's judgment near, or has it already arrived? Can we correlate the national disasters at hand—the floods, tornados, and wildfires—to the mighty hand of God trying desperately to grab our attention? We have taken prayer and God out of our schools. We have taken the Ten Commandments off of public property. Yet we are dismayed when such national disasters occur and have the immaturity to ask, "Why, God?"

Whatever the answer is, we need a believer who understands the power of fasting, who has a national platform, and who has national clout to call for a "Day of Fasting, Humiliation, and Prayer before a Holy and Righteous God," much like our Founding Fathers did many years ago. It is one thing to call for a season of fasting in *word*, but it is a totally separate issue to call a nation to turn from its evil ways and repent of its sins in *action*, much like the king of Nineveh did in the times of Jonah.

It all starts with the church. In Philippians 4:17, the Bible states, "For it is time for the judgment to begin with the family of God." If the church does not step up, how can we expect the unbelieving world to step up? The question is posed, will we have the courage under extreme persecution to turn from our evil ways? As a nation we must never forget from whence we came and above all never forget the promises of God and His Holy Word, much like we find in 2 Chronicles 7:14:

> If my people, who are called by my name,
> Will humble themselves and pray and seek my face
> And turn from their wicked ways,
> Then will I hear from heaven
> And will forgive their sin and will heal their land.

Again, I write in Chapter 17 of *Staving Off Disaster* the following:

It seems as if most Christians have some type of crisis they are dealing with today. It seems as if the Great Restrainer, the Holy Spirit, is being withdrawn from this world, thus allowing sin to run unchecked. What are you struggling with? I look around, and in this world, there is great fear. At the time of this writing, Ebola in America is front and center, the stock market is crashing, ISIS is gaining ground, and enterovirus is sickening our infants. On top of that, our families are fractured, marriages are being dissolved, family businesses are failing, cancer is running rampant, and AIDS and Alzheimer's are killing people around the world.

What about you? What are you struggling with? Is your marriage on the rocks? Do you have a child who has informed you that he or she is gay? Has your only daughter come home and told you she is two months pregnant? Is your business failing? Is the IRS garnishing your wages? Did the rent check bounce? I once had a pastor say, "You are either in a trial, coming out of a trial, or about to enter into one." How true that is!

Both of those excerpts were written and produced four years ago. Some of those issues have changed under the leadership of our current president but much is still front and center.

I categorize those lingering issues into two different levels of problems. Using terminology from my Economics 101 class, I see these as macro problems and micro problems. Macro problems are those dealing with national and global issues that affect us. Micro problems are those dealing with personal and family issues.

If we are living on this side of eternity, we are always going to have problems in this fallen world; and for these problems, we need godly leadership. I believe God has given each of us some level of leadership ability. Do you see yourself as a leader? What are you going to do with what the Lord has given to you?

Let's look at the parable of the talents (Matt 25:14-30). There are three servants listed in that parable. Two of the servants take to heart what the owner has instructed them to do. We don't know the success and failures they had to incur for the investment to double, but that doesn't matter. What does matter is that they tried, and their efforts were blessed for that. The third servant, you'll read, instead dug himself a hole and had no return for the owner's capital.

I believe that each of us have been given some degree of leadership ability. What are you going to do with your portion? Nothing upsets me more than to observe a leader or potential leader who simply sits on the sidelines.

In the 1986 action movie *Top Gun*, we see that Maverick will not engage in a firefight—even when he is most needed—all because he blames himself for the loss of his best friend, Goose, who died in a training accident. Significant human and monetary losses could have occurred had he not fully engaged the enemy. But that is what leaders do. They show up when needed. They engage when needed. And, they step into the batter's box when needed.

In the next chapter we are going to discuss spiritual traits of godly leaders using 1 Corinthians 13. We will discuss how you can sharpen your skills as you live out your faith during these turbulent times.

UNIT 2
LEADERSHIP IS…

Love is patient, love is kind.
It does not envy, it does not boast,
it is not proud.
It is not rude, it is not self-seeking,
it is not easily angered, it keeps no record of
wrongs.
Love does not delight in evil but rejoices with
truth.
It always protects, always trust,
always hopes, always perseveres.
Love never fails.

Apostle Paul

1 Corinthians 13:4-8

CHAPTER 4
LEADERSHIP IS PATIENT

Why is patience at the top of my list of topics to discuss? Well, my personal lack of patience has been something I have struggled with continually in leadership. Back when I was a stockbroker, my impatience offended people, including staff and even clients. When I became a Christian, however, the Holy Spirit would nudge me relentlessly whenever I lost my patience, right up till I fixed it. Making amends and humbling oneself can be exceedingly awkward, and depending on the severity of the wrongdoing, fixing a wrong can be downright painful, too.

The first note to understand is that a lack of patience is rooted in pride. Impatience is all about *self*. It is when your agenda or your time is more important than anyone else's. And, it is when your opinion is more important than anyone else's.

In the late 1980s, I watched a local pastor's impatience sabotage his ministry. His behavior had actually gone on for years before the elders finally stepped in and relieved him of his duties. Later when the pastor humbly came to ask for forgiveness from his staff, it became clear to all that he actually had some bi-polar issues. The pastor then sought help for his condition, to God be the Glory, but not until he lost his ministry and left great personal carnage in his wake. I assume that everyone who had been involved in that situation suffered much pain, both professionally and privately. Thankfully, most of us do not struggle with that level of impatience.

Still, even a small degree of impatience is an outward sign of an *inward* sin issue. And while a person might be able to "get away" with the occasional episode of impatience, that person might notice his or her friends and family having to tiptoe around the elephant in the room if it happens too frequently. That, of course, would be a major sign that one struggles with impatience.

As for me, a verse that speaks to my soul is Proverbs 22:1: "A good name is more desirable than great riches." The good Lord has blessed me with a good name not only within the church community but also among the prison community. I've learned that when I feel impatient, I must ask myself, *Why would I throw all that away for an opportunity to be right? Why would I jeopardize that good name by responding to an email with a short, curt, or rash response to someone?* Any act of impatience is absolutely *not* worth its cost.

To illustrate this concept, think about this: most understand what investments are worth and how hard it is to accumulate them. Would anyone throw a $50,000 stock portfolio out the window? The answer is indubitably "no." A rational person would not do such a thing; however, an impatient person might.

Proverbs 13:2-4 says, "From the fruit of his lips a man enjoys good things, but the unfaithful have a craving for violence. He who guards his lips guard his life, but he who speaks rashly will come to ruin." This is so true. If you are compelled to always speak your mind, you will ultimately damage your relationships. To put it in prison terms, you will be tagged with a bad *jacket*—a vulgar slur implying that when an inmate receives a jacket it is nearly impossible to undo it.

> A patient man has great understanding, but a quick-tempered man displays folly (Prov 14:29).

A hot-tempered man stirs up dissension, but a patient man calms a quarrel (Prov 15:18).

A hot-tempered man must pay the penalty; if you rescue him, you will have to do it again (Prov 19:19).

Do not make friends with a hot-tempered man, do not associate with one easily angered (Prov 22:24).

An angry man stirs up dissension, and a hot-tempered one commits many sins (Prov 29:22).

Along the same lines, Galatians also tackles the issue of impatience. It goes a different direction, however, instead giving us a list of attributes contrary to impatience. In the Galatians 5:22 list, love and patience are used in the same sentence. They are both fruits of the Spirit that Christians should bear.

However, it is difficult to show off these fruits of the Spirit when someone has offended you, making you go from zero to sixty in a nanosecond with hurtful words. Likewise, James chapter 3 also talks about the damage caused by such an untamed tongue. This untamed tongue is an obvious sign of impatience, and most certainly not a fruit of the Spirit.

Such acts of impatience are not uncommon. In fact, some are even predictable. For example, whenever we recruit a team of PFC volunteers for a short-term mission trip, these team members are usually quite unfamiliar with each other at first. Furthermore, they have relatively little time to bond or build relationships before the trips begin. This is coupled with the fact that they will all to soon find themselves in a new land with strange customs. They soon find that their days are long, nights are short and there are no creature comforts to be had. This is a breeding ground for impatient outbursts. Fuses are lit and the next thing you know, *ka-pow*! Someone has said the first thing that popped into their head, and it is hurtful. These kinds of awkward situations are on the leader—so in my case, *me*—for not having adequately trained our teammates on what to expect on a cross-cultural missions trip.

It was after one particularly difficult trip where several of the teammates were at odds with one another that I resolved to put together a training piece to help avoid this in the future. I entitled it *The Power of Three* and it can be found in the appendix under Exhibit A. In it, I talk about five three-word sentences: *Love One Another, Zip Your Lips, Die to Self, Keep Short Accounts, and Build Others Up*. I found that once we started training our people to commit these principles to memory, we minimized the likelihood of people snapping at each other.

We also have another saying taught in our training manual: "Everything is exaggerated when you are on the mission field: emotions, fears, stresses, and other feelings of high anxieties." Experience has shown even the experienced people who usually have their emotions in check may experience moments of high anxiety while in the field. These moments can manifest themselves as a lack of patience towards other teammates. Being on a mission trip will reveal at what level your patience meter resides.

As leaders, we need to model patience and teach others who come behind us to have that same level of commitment. The great love chapter, which covers one of the more difficult Christian skills to master, teaches us that all leaders need to display patience in their lives, publicly as well as privately.

CHAPTER 5
LEADERSHIP IS KIND

Have you ever met a kind person? How did he or she make you feel? Let me tell you about the time I met three of the kindest people within the span of forty-five minutes.

I was on my way home from a PFC training session when I started growing extremely drowsy. We all have had that happen to us on long drives. And what do we try to do when that happens? We try to find the nearest rest stop so that we can take a few minutes to rest our eyes.

However, I had already entered my hometown and had calculated that home was only about five miles away. I told myself that I could make it home. As I got closer, however, I grew more and more tried. The last thing that entered my mind was, "Wow, this is really weird. I am really, really tired," and that was it, lights out.

Of course, the next thing I heard was a loud CRASH. It naturally woke me but I was still virtually comatose. With a firm grip on the wheel and a hill rapidly approaching me, I told myself, "I don't know what happened but I can break and slide softly into this ditch." In my incoherent state, however, what I thought was the brake was actually the *accelerator.*

Witnesses after the event stated that after the first collision, I had actually increased speed. Officers estimated I slammed head-on into the hill going 45 miles an hour. Much to my disgrace, I wasn't wearing a seatbelt either.

Witnesses also stated that I had crossed the center line and had side-swiped a car, sending it into the ditch (explaining what the loud crash had been earlier). In the days after the crash, as I began recalling its events, I realized that I had never before experienced that sensation. Time had felt as if it had actually slowed down. I'd thought I was moving *slowly* towards the hill.

When the first responders arrived to extricate me out of the car, the first EMT who entered the car on the passenger side asked me if I had undone my seat belt.

"I wasn't wearing a seatbelt," I answered.

"Why were you not wearing your seatbelt?" he asked.

And then I started to whimper. He leaned over to me, about three inches from my face, putting his hand on my head and said, "Look at me. Let's not worry about that right now. You are going to be all right. We've got you now."

His words put me completely at ease. This was Kind Person #1!

A second EMT entered the car on the driver's side door. He was there to assess my vital signs, and he did so, explaining what he was doing in a very soft voice, every step of the way. He told me that he was going to put a cervical collar brace on me to stabilize my neck, but before he could do that, he would have to cut off my coat.

I protested. "No, my wife just bought this coat for me a week ago!"

The second EMT gently put his hand on my shoulder and said, "I have to do this. Your wife will understand. It will be ok." Kind Person #2!

As they loaded me into the aid car, a third EMT was busy hooking me up and monitoring my vital signs. She first told me they were going to take me to the nearest hospital. During the drive she leaned over to me, touched my shoulder, and whispered in my ear that there was a change of plans. They were taking me to Harborview, the regional trauma center, which was about a half-hour drive away.

Anyone from our area knew that Harborview was the place you dreaded to hear a loved one was being transported to. During the drive, she asked me if there was anyone she could call for me. She made these calls on my behalf.

Her kindness really shone through when I soon became fidgety. I was strapped down on a board, unable to lift my hands or body. Seeing me struggle, she asked me if everything was okay.

"No, I have an itch," I admitted.

"Where is your itch?" she responded.

"My nose."

She took off her gloves and scratched my nose for me. A few minutes later, however, I started struggling again.

"Same itch?"

"No, but my big toe is itching crazily."

Once again, she took off her rubber gloves and scratched my toe. Kind Person #3!

Three strangers. Three acts of kindness. Three different life examples. Those three strangers taught me about kindness, a gentle touch, a calm, reassuring quiet voice, and acts of service.

That is how I want to be when I grow up. That is how I want to live the remaining years of my life. Because of what *they* taught me, I am always looking to "pay it forward." Look for people who are struggling or having a bad day and see how you may comfort them in their time of need.

Some would say you can't be a strong leader and show acts of kindness. But I disagree. These people also say showing acts of kindness minimizes your leadership authority. I again disagree. I contend that even if you are a boss, responsible for deadlines and budgets, you too can show acts of kindness towards those who report to you. Some would disagree with me and say that you will soon be taken advantage of by those who will abuse your kindness. However, we find an excellent example of a great Leader who never stopped being kind.

The greatest leader who ever walked the earth, Jesus, modeled acts of kindness throughout His ministry. I am reminded of the Samaritan woman at the well in John 4:7-30. Jesus could have not engaged her in a conversation. He could have rebuked her for having five husbands, but He didn't. He engaged her in a conversation. Verses 28-30 state:

> Then, leaving her water jar, the woman went back to the town and said to the people, 'Come, see a man who told me everything I ever did. Could this be the Christ?' *They came out of the town and made their way toward him"* (emphasis added).

Because of Jesus' kindness toward a stranger, the Samaritan woman went back to her town and pointed others to Christ. Similarly, as leaders, we can point others to Jesus through our own acts of kindness.

I am also reminded of the demonic man in Mark 5:1-20. You may know the story. When Jesus gathered His disciples in a boat and crossed the Sea of Galilee, the first person He met was a man plagued by a legion of demons. Out of kindness, Jesus expelled the demons into a herd of pigs. The townspeople came out and were amazed at seeing the once-demon-possessed man sitting, in his right mind and fully-clothed. Comparable to prisoners today, this demon-possessed man was written off by society as being worthless and a throw-away with no worth.

The story didn't end there, either. As Jesus was stepping back into the boat the demon possessed man pleaded with Jesus to allow him to go with Him. But Jesus had other plans.

> As Jesus was getting into the boat, the man who had been demon-possessed begged to go with him. Jesus did not let him, but said, 'Go home to your family and tell them how much the Lord has done for you, and how he has had mercy on you.' So the man went away and began to tell in the Decapolis how much Jesus had done for him. And all the people were amazed (Mark 5:18-20).

After releasing the man from the demons (a truly merciful act of kindness), Jesus told the man to go home to his family and tell them what He had done for him. The demon-possessed man did exactly that. The closing verse to this story says, "And all the people were amazed." A simple act of kindness can point an unbelieving world to Jesus.

There are many other stories that are acts of kindness demonstrated by Jesus; healing the paralytic being lowered from the roof (Matt 9:2-8), cleansing a leper (Mark 1:40-45), healing the women bleeding for twelve years (Mark 5:25-34), and the healing of the lame man at the pool of Bethesda (John 5:1-9).

Jesus took the time to heal people of their physical ailments. While most Christians do not have the gift of healing, we can certainly reach out to a dying world with acts of kindness. Whenever I have failed to be kind to a stranger, I typically blame it on having too little margin in my schedule. I now believe busyness is a tool used by Satan to thwart God's role in our life.

So, what could happen if we slowed down to seek out areas where the Lord could use us in acts of kindness? What would the world be like if Christians endeavored to show more acts of kindness?

I find it interesting that in Galatians 5:22, the fruit of the Spirit, *kindness*, is listed next to *patience*, as we studied in the last chapter. Perhaps it is because as leaders, God expects us to practice those fruits in conjunction with each other.

As a leader, you can attain the ability to be kind by simply practicing kindness. Practicing kindness is similar to building your faith muscle. The more you exercise it, the bigger it becomes and the more it starts to be a part of you.

CHAPTER 6
LEADERSHIP DOES NOT ENVY

Have you ever envied? What causes someone to envy? What *is* envy? Merriam-Webster's dictionary defines envy as "a resentful awareness of an advantage enjoyed by another, joined with a desire to possess the same advantage."[1]

In 1989, Prisoners For Christ was being formed the same time another ministry from my home church was starting. The other ministry was a school for dropouts, for street kids. They were doing a great and admirable work. It was a growing ministry that gathered much praise and public support.

A time came when I petitioned our missions board for a laptop computer to assist me in developing programming for Prisoners For Christ. Several weeks went by and I had not heard back from our missions pastor, and so I thought I would check in on my request. The response I received was that the missions board had run out of time to discuss my proposal for a laptop computer. They also asked me to be patient with them and added that they would respond in the next few weeks.

The week after receiving this response, I bumped into the director of the street school who was sporting her brand-new cell phone. I immediately remembered that I

---

[1]*Merriam Webster,* s.v. "envy," accessed May 14, 2020, https://www.merriam-webster.com/dictionary/envy.

needed a cell phone too, just like hers, to conduct business for Prisoners For Christ. I asked her when and where she got her phone, and she told me all about how blessed she was that the missions board had funded it. *What? They got to her request, but not to mine.* I didn't openly say it and tried to hide my frustration, but I was miffed. Why did they get to her request but not to mine?

I was envious every Sunday after that when I would see her in church with her new phone. I had the sin of covetousness. I was on a slow burn. It started to become a distraction for me every Sunday, and then even throughout the week as I would drive to appointments. It was constantly on my mind. I kept telling myself, *I need a phone too. Why did she receive one and I didn't? What's more, why didn't the missions board discuss my request yet?* What a spoiled little child!

What caused my envy? It was that she had something that I wanted but could not have. It was that I believed that *I* deserved to have a phone as much or even more so than *she* did. It was that *I* was as passionate about inmates hearing the Gospel as she was about street kids, yet she was the one with a phone and I was without. And although I wasn't angry at her per say, my envy was definitely directed toward her.

After several months, I finally heard from the missions board. They had approved my request! Additionally, a donor who was working in the cell phone industry had purchased a phone for the ministry that I could use. I was elated on both fronts. However, because of my attitude in the weeks prior, I now felt that I really did not deserve either gift. Thirty years later, I still remember my disgusting, childlike behavior.

Leaders need to remember that we fight our hardest battles against sin in our thought life. An envious mind not only causes distractions in your daily work life, but it also can wreak havoc on your personal relationships, too.

Envy can run rampant in a new believer as well as a more mature believer. Maybe you have been on the staff of a church for a long time, but your department's budget isn't anywhere near as big as some other departments. Maybe you have been around the church longer than a co-pastor, but he gets more face-time in front of the congregation. Maybe your title isn't as important as the next guy. Be careful! These kinds of envious thoughts can lead you down a path of self-destruction.

Envy is like a large boa constrictor. It slithers in quietly and before you know it, it is crushing your bones, suffocating you! How can you fight envy? You must understand its insidiousness. Understand that envy is *sin*. It is a tool that the enemy uses to seek out and destroy. Proverbs 14:30 says, "A heart at peace gives life to a body, but envy *ROTS* the bones" (emphasis added). Now that is a descriptive statement! How true! The rotting of bones is powerful and accurate metaphor.

Romans 1:28-30 also says, "Furthermore, since they did not think it worthwhile to retain the knowledge of God, he gave them over to a depraved mind, to do what ought to be done. They have become filled with every kind of wickedness, evil, greed and depravity. They are full of *envy*, murder, strife, deceit, and malice. They are gossips, slanderers, God-haters, insolent, arrogant and boastful; they invent ways of doing evil; they disobey their parents" (emphasis added). This word, envy, is mentioned among some of the worst of sins listed in this passage. Envy should never be found in a leader's mind or daily life.

So what's the anecdote for this dangerous snake called envy?

Contentment is the anecdote for envy. The Apostle Paul wrote in Philippians 4:11-12, "I am not saying this because I am in need, for I have learned to be *content* whatever the circumstances. I know what it is to be in need, and I know what it is to have plenty. I have learned the secret of being *content* in any and every situation, whether well fed or hungry, whether living in plenty or in want" (emphasis added). What great instruction from Paul! All leaders need to vaccinate themselves from envy using these words from Paul.

> But godliness with *contentment* is great gain. For we brought nothing into the world, and we can take nothing out of it (1 Tim 6:6-7, emphasis added).

> But if we have food and clothing, we will be *content* with that (1 Tim 6:8. emphasis added).

> Keep your lives free from the love of money and be *content* with what you have, because God has said, "Never will I leave you; never will I forsake you" (Heb 13:5 emphasis added).

> The fear of the Lord leads to life; then one rests *content*, untouched by trouble (Prov 19:23 emphasis added).

If we as leaders don't stamp out envy before it grips our souls, we will fall into a dangerous situation which I call the sin of comparisons. This is when we compare our position in life to someone else's. We may be tempted to work harder or to work longer hours so that we can gain someone's acceptance or advance our position. We may even be tempted to leave a position at the church or ministry because we feel we are not being appreciated. This is when we start relying on our own strength and not the Lord's, and you can see that envy can truly lead us to travel down a road that was not meant for us.

CHAPTER 7
LEADERSHIP IS NOT PROUD

I've had several chances over the years to spend extended periods of time in close quarters with volunteers who have traveled with me to distant prisons. One Sunday, some volunteers and I were driving to Shelton, WA to conduct some PFC-sponsored church services. We left early for the two-hour drive to make it to our first service at 8:30 a.m. On this particular trip, we had the privilege of picking up a new volunteer—something I always enjoyed doing.

We picked up Alex at the nearest park-and-ride, and from the moment Alex entered the car till the time we arrived, he didn't stop talking. I was amazed at how much this man could talk. It was not just that he talked excessively, but that everything out of his mouth was about what *he* had accomplished. He also dropped some prominent names several times in the conversation, which I surmised to be his way of demonstrating his importance. I tried many times to change the subject or divert the subject to someone else in the car, but each time, he brought the conversation back around to himself. I was about ready to say, "Will you please zip your lips?" when I read a highway sign that said Shelton was just five miles away.

Once we unloaded the car, I thought we were off the hook from his endless chatter. We were about to go through security to enter the prison. However, even after security there was a long walk to our first scheduled church service. Alex kept going, nonstop, until we arrived at the prison chapel. I pointed at a chair for him to sit in as I opened our service with a word of prayer.

Alex was all about himself. Few others wanted to work with him. Because he had an uncanny means of quickly developing relationships with the inmates and was a fairly good preacher, I kept him around.

But over the years and months, Alex began rubbing other volunteers the wrong way. He talked a lot. He was a know-it-all. He wasn't a team player. I couldn't put a new person with Alex for fear of Alex running that person off. Alex ultimately left PFC and began bouncing around from ministry to ministry. He eventually started his own prison ministry and was a one-man show. It saddened me to see that a man with such great potential had become so minimized, all because of his pride. I believe there was some baggage from his past life that caused him to be the kind of person he was.

What is the anecdote for being proud?

The Bible says in Proverbs 16:18, "Pride goes before destruction, a haughty spirit before a fall." What is the direct opposite of being proud? Humbleness. There is a direct contrast between being humble of heart and being proud. The Bible speaks against the proud. Let's look towards the Bible to see what it has to say about humbleness.

> You save the humble but bring low those whose eyes are haughty (Ps 18:27).

> He guides the humble in what is right and teaches them his way (Ps 25:9).

> For the Lord takes delight in his people, he crowns the humble with salvation (Ps 149:4).

He mocks proud mockers but gives grace to the humble (Prov 3:34).

God opposes the proud but gives grace to the humble (James 4:6).

In contrast, this is what the Bible says about proud people:

The Lord preserves the faithful, but the proud he pays back in full (Ps 31:23).

Whoever has haughty eyes and a proud heart, him will I not endure (Ps 101:5).

Though the Lord is on high, he looks upon the lowly, but the proud he knows from afar (Ps 138:6).

The Lord detests all the proud of heart. Be sure of this: They will not go unpunished (Prov 16:5).

Haughty eyes and a proud heart, the lamp of the wicked, are sin! (Prov 21:4).

Stuart Scott, in his book *From Pride to Humility,* states,

You cannot have humility where pride exists. Pride is the opposite of humility and it is one of the most loathed sins in God's sight. Pride is an epidemic vice. It is everywhere and manifests itself in many ways.... When someone is proud he or she is focused on self… To sum it all up, proud people believe that life is all about *them*—their happiness, their accomplishments and their worth.[2]

---

[2] Stuart Scott, *From Pride to Humility: A Biblical Perspective* (Bemidji, MN: Focus Pub., 2002), 5.

Every leader should endeavor to never fall into the sin of pride. The Lord gives and the Lord takes away. He builds up and He makes small. Be careful of this insidious and cancerous sin issue. If allowed to run unchecked, pride will destroy your ministry. As someone once said, "A little bit of arsenic in a freshly squeezed glass of orange juice renders the entire glass bad." Leaders need to work on stomping out any form of pride in their life. Never allow it to obtain a foothold.

CHAPTER 8
LEADERSHIP IS NOT RUDE

Think back to the time you heard a rude person spouting off. How did it make you feel? Did you feel sorry for the person who was the target of the outburst? Was it an adult to a child, an adult to another adult? Was it a boss to an employee? Could you determine if it had been a one-time outburst or if the behavior was an ongoing character flaw? Maybe it was a customer to a store clerk or a parent to a child. Regardless of who was being rude, rudeness causes tension for everyone within an earshot of the outburst.

I remember three specific occasions when I have observed rude people going off on other people. The first time was when we had just bought a home in a newly-formed subdivision. Rhonda and I were some of the first homeowners in that neighborhood. I was working from home one day when I heard extremely loud and vulgar language coming from one of the subcontractors working on one of the new homes in the neighborhood. He was obviously having a bad day and taking it out on one of his employees. Every other word he yelled was an expletive. I let it go on until I couldn't take it anymore.

Marching out into the middle of the street, I yelled, "Hey you with the vulgar mouth, dial it back!"

And there was silence for the rest of the day.

The next day, however, he started right back up. This time, though, I didn't wait as long as I had the previous day. For the second time that week, I marched to the front of my house and yelled in an even louder voice, "Hey you with the vulgar mouth! If you don't dial it back I am calling corporate!"

Silence.

I felt sorry for the foreman. I felt sorry for the worker. Obviously, the foreman was having a bad couple of days. Maybe there was something difficult currently going on in his life? Maybe that was how he had been raised? Maybe he had been the target of someone else's tirades growing up? You never know what life circumstances might have shaped the character and behavior of others.

Had I been a more mature Christian at the time, I probably would have walked down to the job site and attempted to reach out to this foreman, to try and minister to his hurting heart. It was obvious that he was under extreme pressure, either at home or at work, maybe both.

The second time I witnessed such blatant rudeness occurred in a grocery store, where I observed a mom raking a child over the coals, not only verbally but physically. I went one way. The mom and the child went the other way. As we met at the opposite end of the store the abuse continued. I was about to step in when another mother intervened, attempting to minister to the mother's heart with a smile and some kindness.

The third situation occurred in a store after Christmas. The store was busy with people returning their unwanted gifts when the customer in front of me went off on the young clerk, who did not approve the customer's returns. The clerk explained that she could not do so because of a new corporate policy requiring receipts. I noticed the clerk at the counter was on the verge of tears.

When it was finally my turn, I spoke softly to the young clerk and said, "You handled that absolutely perfectly. You couldn't have done anything any better. That lady is having a bad day herself. Don't let her bother you. For every one of those angry people, there are twenty more who are appreciative of what you do."

With tears in her eyes she said, "Thank you."

When you see a rude person acting out, you have two opportunities for service. You can minister to the person acting out or you can minister to their target. Which is it going to be? How is the Lord going to lead you? One time it may be to give a kind word to the rude person. Next time it may be comforting the target of the rudeness, as with the young store clerk. Be prepared for either. Ministering to the rude person is tenuous at best. You never know how someone is going to receive your gesture of kindness.

He or she may tell you to, "Take a hike and butt out." However, you might be surprised. Someone may have a tearful meltdown right before your very eyes. That is an excellent time to share the hope we have in Jesus.

I have known Christians who have kind words that roll off their lips when they come face to face with a rude person. Some Christians even carry tracts to hand out to people who are having a bad day. It takes internal strength to seek out those opportunities. When the time comes, and it will, be prepared on all occasions to minister comfort to a hurting soul.

What then is the opposite of rudeness? It is gentleness. Can you guess where *gentleness* is discussed in the Bible? We return to Galatians 5:23 and the fruit of the Spirit. Verse 23 says, "Against such things there is no law." We live in a society full of laws. The speed limit, for example, is a law prohibiting you from going faster than the posted limit.

Regarding the fruit of the Spirit, as explained in Galatians, the Bible says there is no law against these things. In other words, that means "go as fast" as you want in mastering the fruit of the Spirit. Give away as much of that fruit as possible. How would our society change if we all became experts in the fruit of the Spirit?

All of us need to endeavor to receive our PhDs in each of the fruits of the Spirit. What are you going to do today to hone your skills in each of the nine fruits? In each of our respective leadership roles we need to purpose to display kindness and not rudeness to those who come behind us. Displaying rudeness is not a quality befitting a Christian leader.

CHAPTER 9
LEADERSHIP IS NOT SELF-SEEKING

It is never a good idea to have *self* involved in any activity or relationship because *self* is rooted in pride—this much is seen in the relationships of today, all the way back to the fall of man where it began. We endanger ourselves when we focus on *self,* because becoming self-absorbed turns a person inward to the desires of the flesh and the mind.

In the movie *Spiderman 3*, the young Peter Parker succumbs to his dark desires, allowing a dark black suit to replace his red Spiderman suit. This black suit is able to give him powers stronger than he could have ever imagined, enticing him to let it take over. When that happens, the dark power of the suit invades his entire being and soon, Peter realizes that he is unable to take off the black suit by himself. The black suit and its evil has become part of him.

When Peter comes to his senses, he attempts to take it off. His efforts are now in vain as the black suit refuses to comply. No matter how hard Peter pulls and stretches the suit, it always snaps back into place, molding back into shape on his body. Peter soon realizes that he is powerless against the suit and that there is nothing he can do to release him from the hold that the black suit has on him.

Peter eventually perches himself on top of a church where he wrestles with the darkness until he finally rips it off, freeing him. Peter collapses to the ground in exhaustion, free at last.

This scene is a great metaphor for what we risk when we allow the desires of self to control us. When darkness seeps in and takes over, we find that we cannot rid ourselves of it in our own power. 1 John 2:15-17 states:

> Do not love the world or anything in the world. If anyone loves the world, the love for the Father is not in him. For everything in the world—the cravings of sinful man, the lust of his eyes, and the boastings of what he has and does—comes not from the Father but from the world. The world and its desires pass away, but whoever does the will of God lives forever.

This is what self is all about. Once we allow the lust of the flesh, the lust of the eyes, and the pride of heart to ensnare us, we become all about satisfying *self*. Once we allow self to entice us, it is no different than when Peter Parker *allowed* the more powerful black suit to take over his red one. We cannot break the dark hold of self with our own power. If we continue in the darkness of self, we may end up in the gutter, in prison, or somewhere even worse. When we give in to the sin of satisfying self, life is not being lived as the Almighty has planned for us.

> When tempted, no one should say, "God is tempting me." For God cannot be tempted by evil, nor does he tempt anyone; but each one is tempted when, by his own evil desire, he is dragged away and enticed. Then, after desire has conceived, it gives birth to sin; and sin, when it is full-grown, gives birth to death (James 1:13-15).

What an incredible word picture James paints. Instead of being self-seeking, we should be God-seeking.

> But mark this: There will be terrible times in the last days. People will be lovers of themselves, lovers of money, boastful, proud, abusive, disobedient to their parents, ungrateful, unholy, without love, unforgiving, slanderous, without self-control, brutal, not lovers of the good, treacherous, rash, conceited, lovers of pleasure rather than lovers of God—having a form of godliness but denying its power. Have nothing to do with them (2 Tim 3:1-5).

As leaders in the King's army, His Green Berets, His Navy Seals, we should never be self-seeking but instead be God-seeking. So, if you have a sliver of *self* attempting to gain control of you, I want you to stop, drop to your knees, and rebuke that evil spirit in the Name of Jesus! Be on guard and fight the good fight!

CHAPTER 10
LEADERSHIP IS NOT EASILY ANGERED

Rudeness and anger fit hand in glove. Chapter 8 of this work discusses the topic of rudeness, outlining the three occasions of when I witnessed rudeness happening—the construction foreman to his work crew, the lady to her child in the grocery store, and the customer to the clerk at Christmas. There is a common denominator in these three stories: two people were involved in each situation—first, a dominant person, and second, a subservient person. Each of these dominant persons was rude to the subservient person. One may even deduce from these stories that these dominant persons were probably angry human beings who lived angry lives. At least, that is what these episodes had demonstrated to me. In each situation, they had bullied those whom they perceived were of lesser social statures.

Now, anger usually flows downhill to someone of perceived lesser value. It rarely flows uphill. For example, you do not often see an angry person "taking it out" on someone of higher life stature. This doesn't mean that it never happens, but that it is less common. Considering this, does that mean angry people are born the way they are? Or does it mean they become that way because of life circumstances? I suspect 99% of angry people in the world become that way because of life circumstance. History has already proven that some abused children grow up being angry people. The sad truth is that these children often end up becoming what they have despised their entire lives.

There are other reasons behind angry people, such as disappointments in jobs, broken relationships, or simply too many failures in life. Some have experienced failed dating and marriage relationships. Some even add bitterness to their anger when their poor choices in life lead to severe consequences. And of course, the sudden loss of a loved one due to an illness or accident may change a person's temperament forever, too. Sometimes anger is even produced by a medical condition, such as those who suffer with bi-polar disorders, though there are prescription drugs that can help with these disorders today.

The point is to understand this: there is almost AL-WAYS a backstory to someone's anger no matter what the cause is for one's anger. Understand this: many times, angry and bitter people tend to beget other angry and bitter people.

In the past, I'll admit that I have had bursts of rudeness and anger myself. I've learned that only through the renewing of the mind can one overcome that kind of behavior. When I was younger, my anger was directed outward towards people or inanimate objects. When I had that under control, however, my anger shifted inward, nestling within the quietness of my mind. Neither type of anger was good for me. Anger is *destructive*, regardless of where it is directed.

Anger also tends to attach itself to its master. It is no different than when the black Spiderman suit that wouldn't relinquish its subject, Peter Parker. Much like an eagle sinking its talons deep into its prey, so goes anger when one allows it to fester.

The Bible has also much to say about anger:

A gentle answer turns away wrath, but a harsh word stirs up anger (Prov 15:1).

Do not make friends with a hot-tempered man, do not associate with one easily angered (Prov 22:24).

For as churning the milk produces butter, and as twisting the nose produces blood, so stirring up anger produces strife (Prov 30:33).

And do not grieve the Holy Spirit of God, with whom you were sealed for the day of redemption. Get rid of all bitterness, rage, and anger, brawling and slander, along with every form of malice. Be kind and compassionate to one another, forgiving each other, just as in Christ God forgave you (Eph 4:30-32).

You used to walk in these ways, in the life you once lived. But now you must rid yourselves of all such things as these: anger, rage, malice, slander, and filthy language from your lips (Col 3:7-8).

Thus, a leader should never be prone to angry outbursts. In Chapter 4, I shared the story of a local pastor who lost his ministry because he was unable to control his anger. The consequences are almost always unavoidable for one with such uncontrolled anger. Anger can cause anyone to lose everything.

What is the antidote for anger?

Any malady that is not God-honoring needs to be dealt with or it will cause you great pain, in both your personal and professional relationships. Romans 12:1-2 is the key to securing a firm grip on anger as it is all about the renewing of the mind.

Therefore, I urge you, brothers, in view of God's mercy, to offer your bodies as living sacrifices, holy and pleasing to God—this is your spiritual act of worship. Do not conform any longer to the pattern of this world, but be transformed by the renewing of your mind. Then you will be able to test and approve what God's will is—his good, pleasing and perfect will (Rom 12:1-2).

There are three keys to understanding this Scripture:

Key #1: In this passage the Bible says to "offer your body as a living sacrifice holy and pleasing to God." Paul uses an interesting set of words—*a living sacrifice*. This is totally contrary to what the Jewish nation had been accustomed to at the time. They were accustomed to animal sacrifices. What does Paul mean by a living sacrifice? Some scholars believe a living sacrifice means giving your life totally to God while you are alive. That can be interpreted as an unconditional surrender to God and to His designs for your life. As leaders, I believe we need to take hold of this concept of unconditional surrender.

Key #2: In Romans 12, the Bible speaks of the patterns of the world. What are the patterns of this world? It is this: refusing to give in to society's pressures and norms. But how can we inoculate ourselves from those pressures while still living among them? Well, it is difficult if we are not intentional about it. However, the more we read our Bible, the more we have quality quiet times, the more our lives start transforming each day. The more we practice good spiritual disciplines, the more we do this inch by inch, yard by yard, and mile by mile, the more we will not conform to the patterns of this world.

Key #3: Be transformed by the renewing of your mind. This is the grand prize, the whole enchilada, the jumbo dog in the baseball park, the complete renewing of your mind to the things of God and not the things of the world.

As leaders, we need to strive to have a complete renewing of the mind—a godly "brain transplant." We need to hear from God daily amid the commotion that surrounds us in everyday life. It is not easy. Satan is always crouching at our mind's doorstep to tempt us, to ensnare, and to drag us off using our own temptations. Once that is complete, he then demeans and belittles us until we stumble. But remember this Church—Romans 8:37 says you are more than conquerors.

CHAPTER 11
LEADERSHIP KEEPS NO RECORD OF WRONGS

In the mid-eighties, several years after our conversion experience, my wife and I had some "intense fellowship" (also known as a spirited disagreement). In the heat of our discussion, she rattled off seven different deficiencies in me—instances that had occurred ten years prior to this disagreement. It stopped me in my tracks, leaving me speechless. I was stunned for many different reasons. *She is wrong on so many different levels*, I had thought to myself. I was shocked that these things still bothered her.

When I finally got over the shock, I started to wonder, *How did she do that? How did she fire off that list so quickly?* I wondered if there was some hidden list she had been keeping, memorizing, and saving for such a time as *this*. Where was this list, and how could I get to it?

I'm thankful to say that over the course of time in our marriage, the list-keeping has pretty much disappeared. (Thank you, Jesus!) It is either because she now has trained her husband perfectly, which we know is far from accurate, or because she has grown in her own spiritual walk. I know the latter to be true. My wife has grown immensely in her spiritually walk over the years.

Now ladies, please don't write me any hate mail. Don't judge me on the forthcoming. I have observed over the years that ladies struggle with list-making the most. Not to say that men don't make lists of their own, of course. I have definitely known some men who have perfected their own system of list-keeping, too.

What can you do once your behavior has caused these trust issues in others? To stop list-keeping of other's sins, we need to work on four areas. First, you need to have a salvation experience with Christ Jesus. My mind quickly jumps to Romans 10:9-10 which states "that if you confess with your mouth, Jesus is Lord, and believe in your heart that God raised him from the dead, you will be saved." That is the beginning of anyone's new walk with the Lord. It all starts with trusting Jesus for your salvation.

Second, you need to understand and *believe* that you are a new creation. Once the salvation issue is resolved, I am reminded of 2 Corinthians 5:17 which states, "Therefore, if anyone is in Christ, he is a new creation; the old has gone, the new has come." I must remember that because I am now in Christ, by believing in Him and Him alone for my salvation, I am a new man. This is exhilarating news. I have been washed with the blood of the Lamb. The old man is gone, and the new man is here. You should be as excited as I am for this revelation—*you* are now a new creation!

There often comes a problem with this understanding, however. That problem is that the old man will keep wanting to rear its ugly head back in your life. When your old man starts rising up, sin issues will start piling up, too. Your relationships will get bruised, and you may even find that family and friends have begun keeping records of your wrongdoings. You might even notice others breaking off their relationships with you because they don't fully trust that your old man is dead—more importantly, that he is going to stay dead.

This brings us to the third key, which is that you must commit to publicly declaring that the new man is alive and thriving. Over time, people will notice and say, "Something is different about you. What's changed?"

Fourth, you must renew your mind. Commit to reading God's Word daily. Once you learn what the "owner's manual" (the Bible) has to say about how we should be living our lives, we then get to make a choice—do we believe the Bible or not? If we *do* believe it, then we need to put it into action, daily. Remember Romans 12:1-2 says:

> Therefore I urge you, brothers, in *view* of God's mercy, to offer your bodies as living sacrifices, holy and pleasing to God—this is your spiritual act of worship. Do not conform any longer to the patterns of this world, but be transformed by the *renewing of your mind*. Then you will be able to test and approve what God's will is—his good, pleasing and perfect will (emphasis added).

As you go through these steps, there might be days where you need comfort. Psalm 103:11-12 brings me great comfort. It says, "For as high as the heavens are above the earth, so great is his love for those who fear him; as far as the east is from the west, so *far has he removed our transgressions* from us" (emphasis added). That should bring you incredible comfort, too. This verse says that the Lord, the Creator of the universe, remembers not our sins. Similarly, a New Testament verse that also says this is Romans 8:1-2: "Therefore, there is now no condemnation for those who are in Christ Jesus, because through Christ Jesus, the law of the Spirit of life set me free from the law of sin and death." To this day, I vividly remember the first time the enormity of that verse hit me. It was at the life group I discussed in Chapter 2.

While I'm writing about the sin of list-keeping, I'd like to explain why it is a topic I tend to hover over. I came from a Catholic background, and as you may know, Catholics are encouraged to go to confession each Saturday. As a Catholic, you are one day "in the Kingdom" if you have been good, but the next day you could be "out" if you commit mortal sins and neglect to confess them—at least until a priest gives you absolution.

When Christ came into my life, I realized I didn't have to go to a priest here on earth anymore. I could go directly to my Father in heaven for the forgiveness of my sins. This realization brought me great freedom, because I now knew that I had a loving Father—a Father who promised me that once I'd accepted His Son and confessed my sin, He would remember my sin no more. The reality of it is that as believers, our sins are now as far away as the east is from the west. But the enemy does not want us to believe that truth. Instead, he wants to throw the guilt of our sins at us daily, reminding us of what destitute and despicable people we are.

Isaiah 43:25 reads, "I, even I, am he who *blots* out your transgressions, for my own sake, and remembers your sins no more" (emphasis added). It really doesn't get much clearer than that. Isaiah states that our sins are totally blown up and annihilated so there are never any remains of them. This is a promise we can hold onto tightly and should bring you great comfort. Here are some other verses that speak along the same lines:

> Come now, let us reason together, says the Lord. Though your sins are like scarlet, they shall be as white as snow (Is 1:18).

> We all, like sheep, have gone astray, each of us has turned to our own way; and the Lord has laid on him the iniquity of us all (Is 53:6).

I would be remiss if I didn't bring up two points while we are on this topic. First, although our sins are forgiven, these verses do not give us a free license to go out and sin recklessly. In fact, Romans 6:1-4 speaks against doing that. Second, although our sins are forgiven, there still may be physical consequences of those past sins. For example, if you were an alcoholic or a drug abuser, you may have done significant damage to your body. If you were sexually promiscuous, you may have contracted HIV or an STD. If you were a violent individual, you may be serving time in a jail or prison. But no matter who you are, know this: regardless of what you may have done in your past life, if you are now in Christ Jesus, He is right there with you now.

The whole point I'm making here is that if the Lord does not keep track of *our* sins, then why do we keep track of others' wrongdoings? The answer is simple—it comes down to our pride problem. We want to be right. Also, we may not have truly forgiven people of their offenses against us. We may even be tucking away their offenses so that we can use them at some point in the future.

If you're a leader in the making, I encourage you to throw away the mental lists of those who have offended you. Truly forgive those who have caused you great pain. I know some betrayal pain cuts very deep, but as Christians, we are required to forgive, or we will not receive forgiveness ourselves (Matt 6:15). Remember, those who do not forgive are in bondage. Forgiveness is as much for the person being hurt as it is for the transgressor. Also, if you haven't fully forgiven someone, you are living exactly as Satan wants you to live, consumed by bitterness. That is not God's plan for your life.

This also reminds me of the parable of the unjust servant in Matthew 18:23-35. This is the story of a servant who owed his master ten thousand talents but could not pay.

Some say this amount of money in today's dollars equates to billions or some other insurmountable amount. The servant fell at the feet of his master and pleaded with him to be patient. The master took pity on the servant and forgave his debt.

That first servant then went out and found one of his own fellow servants who also owed him a hundred denarii, which equaled to about a hundred days of average pay. This second servant, much like the first servant, fell to his knees and pleaded for mercy. But instead of extending mercy to this second servant as his own master had shown to him, the first servant instead threw the second servant in prison. He failed to extend the same mercy he had received for a much larger debt.

This story illustrates what we sometimes do, too. Sometimes we are ungrateful for what the Lord has done for us—going to the cross to pay the debt of our sin. When we talk about the forgiveness of our sins and the unmerited grace extended to us, we should always remember this parable.

Furthermore, we should remember this parable when we talk about never keeping record of wrongdoings. Jesus, through His death and resurrection, has already paid the ultimate price for you and me to receive the mercy that we don't deserve. In working through our relationships, both personal and professional, a leader needs to practice keeping no record of wrongdoings. We should strive to enter into every interaction as if nothing has ever offended you. Keep this at the forefront of your mind. Remember what has been forgiven of you!

A word for bosses in the secular workplace

If you are a boss with employees, you may feel as if you are walking a fine line when it comes to list-keeping. This is where biblical principles often seem to clash with the world's system. We live in a litigious society. If you are a boss or a supervisor, you have the responsibility to document bad work performance or insubordination so that if you are ever called to justify a termination, you will be able to defend your position. Documenting and terminating an employee for poor job performance is not the same as keeping a record of personal offenses.

If you have been working on living out the first two chapters, *Leadership is Patient* and *Leadership is Kind*, you will be able to explain, in a professional and kind manner, the ways in which an employee's performance is lacking and how it needs to be addressed. A termination should never come as a surprise to anyone. If you have done your job as a leader, you will have already explained the expectations. If those expectations are not met, then it is up to you to set the person on the right path with a clearly defined plan for correction. I believe in giving people second and third chances. If work performance continues to miss the mark, it would be best for you to "bless that employee" out of your organization.

When that happens, it is critical to review your interviewing process. I am a firm believer that one hundred percent of the time, employee problems can be headed off in the interviewing process. This is a key factor in developing a high functioning "dream team." You not only need to hire for the skill set, you also need to hire for the culture of your organization. If you make a mistake in hiring just for a skill set without any thought to the culture of your team, you are only inviting disaster.

CHAPTER 12
LEADERSHIP DOES NOT DELIGHT IN EVIL

In the formative years of Prisoner For Christ, I knew nothing, about nothing—Christian ministry, working in the jails, working with board members, or maintaining an energized volunteer base. Every day, I simply endeavored to put one foot in front of the other as I navigated the many twists and turns that came with ministry. I was thirty-four years old when we finally received the blessing of our church elders to start the prison ministry. We were exhilarated, because it had seemed like a new ministry was starting every month in this large church Rhonda and I were attending in those days. It was finally our turn, and excitement hung in the air every Sunday morning as we told everyone who would listen about the blessings of being a volunteer in the prison ministry.

However, I knew nothing about the inner workings of a large church. I wanted pulpit time a couple times per quarter. I wanted a ministry booth out in the lobby every week. I wanted all the PFC brochures in the church's brochure rack. I quickly learned, through some disappointments, that these things were not going to happen. I was so naïve.

As other ministries started, I began to feel jealous. As mentioned before, the sin of envy is insidious. One may even find that envy can cause you to hope that others will struggle. It is an easy leap for you to delight in their struggles or setbacks. This is the thought life of an immature believer. This attitude should never be in the heart of a believer. Then how did it happen to me?

As believers, we need to be aware and watch for this wrongful progression in attitude. These are the stages of jealousy a leader in ministry may experience: starting a ministry, excitement in the new ministry, comparing the ministry to other ministries, jealousy of other ministries, desiring them to struggle, and finally delighting in the problems of other ministries. This downward spiral can be traced back to our sin of pride.

While God-given passion is something to be celebrated, you must still be careful with it! Do not let that excitement blind you, ultimately leading you down the dark path I've described above.

Remember, leadership does not delight in evil!

Leadership never hastily assigns sinister intent or nefarious motivations to another. True and godly leadership resists the temptation to pass judgement.

You should never focus on another's sin issues, wrongdoings, or shortcomings. We all walk around in the flesh, and we all have sin issues. We all have leadership issues, too. Instead of focusing on those issues, focus on your own growth instead. We should feel sorrowful whenever sin or personal failings take place; we should never rejoice because someone has fallen.

In the past, when I have seen others engage in sin, I have had thoughts like, "Lord, fry that man!" or "That man needs a good dose of the Lord's correction." When those thoughts invade our brains, we need to immediately tell ourselves, "No! Stop that!" These thoughts are straight from the enemy.

Rather, as leaders, we should always have a spirit of help, of service, and of being a "cheerleader" for those in other ministries. This is why I will always make time to talk to someone from another ministry, to exchange ideas with them, and share what I have learned. I want to build others up in ministry by sharing what God has shown me, including sharing about my past mistakes.

Every year, I receive a number of calls from people wanting advice on how to start a nonprofit, on how to fundraise, on how to manage teams, and even about how to start a prison ministry. If I were insecure, I would not take any of those calls—especially the calls from those who may start a competing prison ministry. Instead, I choose to make time for them. I remind myself that this is all about discipleship. *Each one, teach one!* I believe that as leaders, we need to hold loosely our successes and our failures, willing to share both, to build up the Body of Christ. Don't be afraid of being transparent with your own shortcomings.

In the early years of Prisoners For Christ, people freely shared their ministry and leadership experiences with me, for which I am eternally grateful. I was often amazed at the materials and guidance that some sent my way. They "got it." They understood the concept of openly sharing both their strengths and weaknesses. I will say it again: Leadership does not delight in evil!

> True love [Leadership] rejoices in what is right and good. Anything that covers up sin or seeks to justify wrongdoing is the polar opposite of godly love. Love [Leadership] does not sweep sin under the rug. Love [Leadership] does not try to find ways to get away with bad behavior, and it does not put up with injustice. Instead, it treasures truth, celebrates good behavior, and promotes virtue. True love [Leadership] has nothing to hide.

> Further, to "not delight in evil" carries the idea of not gloating over someone else's guilt. It is common for people to rejoice when an enemy is found guilty of a crime or caught in a sin. This is not love. Love [Leadership] rejoices in the virtue of others, not in their vices. Sin is an occasion for sorrow, not for joy.[3]

Instead, true godly leadership delights in what is right and good. Leadership desires truth. As we become more Christ-like, we need to grow in our leadership strengths by maximizing our giftedness while minimizing our weaknesses.

We can do this by vaccinating ourselves from the covetousness that is sometimes prevalent within our churches and Christian organizations. Do the best job you can do in the area where God has planted you. Help others. Do not compete for attention. Do not delight in someone's struggles. Pray for those who come behind you or who need your advice. Give that advice freely. Don't hold back.

Being a Christian leader, however, does not mean you sweep issues under the carpet when staff underperforms, complains, or has moral failures. Leadership engages in godly confrontation when needed. It does no one any good to ignore problems in employees. What would have happened to Moses if he had not confronted Korah and his men about their rebellious spirit? In fact, not dealing with issues right away can have a longer-term negative effect for all involved. A leader corrects and a leader teaches. A leader explains expectations. A leader seeks the truth on all occasions.

---

[3] GotQuestions.org, "Home," GotQuestions.org, November 14, 2012, https://www.gotquestions.org/love-not-delight-evil-rejoices-truth.html.

CHAPTER 13
LEADERSHIP ALWAYS PROTECTS

What does the Bible mean when it says "love always protects?" Psalm 91:14 is a good starting point to answering that question. It reads, "'Because he loves me,' says the LORD, 'I will rescue him; I will protect him, for he acknowledges my name.'" Psalm 91 has been a great source of encouragement for saints through the centuries. In times of calamity, the Lord speaks to us through His Holy word. The Lord begins with, "Because he loves me." As believers, we are to love the Lord with all our heart, mind, and soul. The Bible is a place of rest with promises for those who love Him. Below is a sampling of verses that speak of the Lord's protection.

> For the LORD your God moves about in your camp to protect you and to deliver your enemies to you. Your camp must be holy, so that he will not see among you anything indecent and turn away from you (Deut 23:14).

> The hand of our God was on us, and he *protected* us from enemies and bandits along the way (Ezra 8:31, emphasis added).

> But let all who take refuge in you be glad; let them ever sing for joy. Spread your *protection* over them, that those who love your name may rejoice in you (Ps 5:11, emphasis added).

71

O LORD, you will keep the needy safe and protect us forever from such people forever (Ps 12:7).

You are my hiding place; you will *protect* me from trouble and surround me with songs of deliverance (Ps 32:7, emphasis added).

The LORD will protect him and preserve his life; he will bless him in the land and not surrender him to the desire of his foes (Ps 41:2).

For he guards the course of the just and protects the way of his faithful ones (Ps 2:8).

My prayer is not that you take them out of the world but that you protect them from the evil one (John 17:15).

But the Lord is faithful, and he will strengthen you and protect you from the evil one (2 Thess 3:3).

As a leader, you are called to protect those in your charge, as the Lord protects His faithful ones. Likewise, the head of a household is called to protect his wife and children. You may ask, "Protect them from what?" Protect them from the influences from the outside world. Protect them from making bad choices, protect them from their friends, and protect them from the evil influences that bombard our homes daily.

As a boss, you are called to protect your team. You are called to move your corporate objectives forward. You need to protect your team from petty fights, from gossip, from divisive individuals, and from outside negativity. You are also to protect them from making bad decisions that could derail the progress of your team.

Fifteen years ago, I realized that if I were to expand the ministries of PFC around the world, I would need fully-trained International Group Leaders (IGLs). Leading a prison team to another part of the world is very different than leading a team of volunteers to a local jail on the home front. Many things can quickly go wrong on the international mission field. Therefore, we instituted an extensive training program for individuals who are called to be IGLs. This program has several phases of growth: Assistant Team Leader, Co-team Leader, Senior Team Leader with a shadow, Senior Team Leader, and lastly, a Four-Star Team Leader. This gives the ministry confidence that individuals who have progressed through this training should confidently be able to lead a missions trip.

A new IGL is required to lead a team with a shadow. This shadow is a person who is senior to the IGL. The shadow is basically "along for the ride," and his role is to only speak when asked for guidance, or when he or she thinks the team is making decisions that could cause problems. Whenever I am a shadow, I stay silent, but I listen closely to the team as they make decisions. I provide guidance and input when needed, with the objective of protecting the team as well as growing their leadership skills.

In the police and the military forces there is the saying, "I got your six." What does that mean? It actually originated in WWI as a line that soldiers would say to one another. The number six corresponds to the hour on the clock and meaning, "I have your back." True leaders should always have the backs of those they love, those they care for, and those they work with. In a sense, this is a biblical principle. The Bible says several times that the Lord is our rear guard. A rear guard is to defend from attacks from behind that which an army cannot see. Knowing the Lord is my rear guard and has my back, or "has my six", is extremely comforting. True godly leaders always protect their people by being their rear guard.

The Pendulum

The practice of leaders providing protection for those in their charge requires balance. It is like a pendulum. If the pendulum swings too far in the direction of zero protection, there will be no confidence that the leader is watching out for the team's wellbeing. If the pendulum swings too far in the direction of over-protection, it will foster an environment that allows poor behavior to continue. Be sure your leadership pendulum is balanced in the middle of these two extremes.

CHAPTER 14
LEADERSHIP ALWAYS TRUSTS

I often say to my staff and my key volunteers, "I trust you impeccably." What do I mean? I mean, "You are fully trained. I have watched you make decisions. Go and make the best decisions you can make on behalf of the ministry. I trust you impeccably."

The leadership skill of trust is a double-edged sword. When staff come to you and tell you that they have made a mistake, you cannot overreact, or they will be gun shy of ever making another decision within the organization. Obviously, some staff are going to have better decision-making skills than others. Those with more experience will be more confident in their own decision-making. The trust you have in your employees is also built over time and experience.

This is the way I look at it: If a staff member has a track record of making good decisions ninety percent of the time, I also expect that person will make bad decisions the other ten percent of the time. To me, that is a grand slam employee. That person rocks. I expect losses. Granted, some losses cost more than others.

When staff members come to me, clearly uncomfortable with what they need to say, I sometimes must "prime the pump" and get the conversation started. I will kindly start with, "What's going on? Talk to me." Once I can establish a calm and comfortable atmosphere, it is much easier for them to tell me about their mistakes. It is my job to put their minds at ease and help them determine the next proper course of action. In the last thirty plus years of ministry, no mistake has yet taken down the ministry.

When it comes to employee mistakes, I have observed that there are four different types. The first is the awkward mistake, a type of relationship mistake. This is when an interaction with a volunteer, a donor, or some other ministry constituent has gone wrong. The second type of mistake is the costly financial mistake. For example, one time a staffer who was on her first day with the ministry ruined a copier drum, which cost us $500 in repairs. She was terribly upset about it, but I comforted her and told her the Lord would handle it. The third kind of mistake is one that makes you flop your head on your desk with a big sigh. I have experienced two of those mistakes over the years. Guess what? We survived both, and I can now smile about them years later. Fourth is the "deer in the headlights" mistake. These are the mistakes that startle you with their foolishness. These are the ones that require you to have the self-control not to say, "What were you thinking?" As a leader, you need to carefully work through this kind of mistake with your staffer.

There are several responses and solutions you can have to employee mistakes. First, you might just tell your employees to handle it themselves. Second, you might ask the individual, "What do you think are the possible solutions? What would *you* do to fix it?" You can then discuss the possible solutions, coming to an agreement and instructing the person to carry on giving you updates as needed. Third, you can tell staff to back away from the problem and let you handle it. Sometimes problems can only be fixed by the leader and not the person who committed the mistake. When this course of action needs to occur, it is often a huge time-investment for the leader. I'll admit, I hate becoming involved in problems caused by others. I prefer staff members handle their own problems. While mistakes can be costly, replacing staff costs even more.

If you have a team you believe in, none of these mistakes are grounds for termination unless they involve blatant insubordination, fraud, or a moral failing. A mistake that may be grounds for termination is if something in your employee's private life is so egregious that it makes the news reflecting poorly on your organization. Mistakes that are repeated time and time again may also be reason for termination because your staffer has shown he or she is not teachable.

When it comes to teaching leaders, I also like to tell them about the "Moses approach" to management. In Exodus 18, Moses' father-in-law, Jethro, observes Moses working long hours. He pulls Moses aside to give him some advice. Jethro says, "What you are doing is not good. You and these people who come to you will only wear yourselves out. The work is too heavy for you; you cannot handle it alone" (Ex 18:17-18).

Jethro did a great job in pointing out a weakness in Moses' leadership. However, he doesn't just point out a flaw, but gives Moses some solid solutions. He says in verse 21, "But select capable men from all the people—men who fear God, trustworthy men who hate dishonest gain—and appoint them as officials over thousands, hundreds, fifties and tens" (emphasis added).

Regardless of the times, be it Moses' times or in the twenty-first century, you will find that the process of building up trustworthy men and women has not changed. As a leader, you observe. You train. You observe some more. You inspect. You correct. You promote. Then you cut them loose to make their own decisions. You'll find in

Scripture that even in Moses' time, the exceptionally difficult or critical decisions needed to be brought to the leader.

Below are some additional Scriptures that show the importance of finding people who are trustworthy:

> Altogether, those chosen to be gatekeepers at the thresholds numbered 212. They were registered by genealogy in their villages. The gatekeepers had been assigned to their positions of *trust* by David and Samuel the seer (1 Chron 9:22, emphasis added).

> I put Shelemiah the priest, Zadok the scribe, and a Levite named Pedaiah in charge of the storerooms and made Hanan son of Zaccur, the son of Mattaniah, their assistant, because these men were considered *trustworthy*. They were made responsible for distributing the supplies to their brothers (Neh 13:13, emphasis added).

> The Lord detests lying lips, but he delights in men who are truthful (Prov 12:22).

Finally, leadership always trusts. Being a trusting leader does not mean you are a doormat. Some may take advantage of your trust, but I firmly believe that if you hire correctly, train correctly, and allow adequate time for staff to earn trust, those who take advantage will be the exception and not the rule.

The Pendulum

Something to note when it comes to trust is that if the pendulum of trust swings too far in the no-trust-at-all direction, you will breed an environment of fear and suspicion.

You will squash all initiative causing your staff to be wary of your leadership. If all decisions, large or small, *need* to be run by you, you will soon be labeled as a control freak, as a micro-manager. Furthermore, if you foster an environment of too much control, you will only wear out both yourself and your staff. Also note that most staff will only put up with this for so long. You will soon have a high workforce turnover rate, which will then stunt the organization's momentum. Additionally, the time, training, and overall investment costs of hiring will be staggering.

However, if the pendulum should swing too far the *other* way—where trust is blind with no verification—you will have staff taking advantage of your naivety. I once had a good friend, Don Szolomayer, teach me a very valuable lesson about this. He told me, "Von Tobel, you need to INSPECT what you EXPECT." What incredibly wise advice. I have used that motto for over fifteen years now.

If you inspect too much, that also can be problematic. That is sending a message to your employees that you don't trust them. As leaders, we need to be reminded daily that leadership always protects and always trusts.

If being over-controlling is something you struggle with, it can be hard work to break that habit. Here is what you should do: First, become familiar with the Moses approach to delegation. Next, commit to pray daily that the Lord will give you the grace you need to trust people. Then, identify your fears determining how to mitigate those fears. Identify employees who are strong and capable, who only need minimal instruction, as well the ones who might need more frequent input. If your corporate success depends on *their* success in managing their tasks, then you will want to inspect what you expect more frequently. Be diligent in finding the right balance.

CHAPTER 15
LEADERSHIP ALWAYS HOPES

What does hope mean to the unsaved world? The reference website Bible Study Tools defines *hope* as, "To trust in, wait for, or desire something or someone; or to expect something beneficial in the future."[4] Merriam-Webster's online dictionary also defines *hope* as, "to cherish a desire with anticipation: to want something to happen or be true."[5] These are the world's definitions of hope.

When people become sick with life threatening illnesses, such as cancer or heart disease, they place their hope in the hands of doctors and specialists. Family and friends hope for their loved ones to have a speedy recovery. When businesses face major problems, business owners hope for a solution that will minimize financial damages. When a pandemic hits our world, there is hope that scientists will develop a cure and a vaccine. When parents send a child off to college, they hope for the best for that child, and for that child to be safe. When people buy lottery tickets, they are hoping to win "the big one." Some say hope only comes into play in a crisis, but I disagree.

Many times, people confuse hope with *wishful thinking.* There is a huge difference between the two. Hope is placed in the hands of those who have the power to solve the

---

[4] Bible Study Tools, s,v., "hope," accessed May 16, 2020, https://www.biblestudytools.com/dictionary/hope.

[5] *Merriam Webster,* s.v., "hope," accessed May 16, 2020, https://www.merriam-webster.com/dictionary/hope.

problem, as with the doctors solving a critical health problem. Wishful thinking is usually based on a longshot or unrealistic dreams, like the odds of holding the winning lottery ticket. Wishful thinking is the development of ideological outcomes that are pleasing to the mind, like a get-rich-quick scheme or a pyramid scheme.

All hope without God in the equation is no hope at all; it is false hope. God created us to have emotions—joy, gratitude, empathy, and contentment to name a few. Hope is one of those emotions that is truly rooted in the Bible. God created us to have our hope in Him. Satan and the world's version of "hope" is a poor imitation of what God created for us.

What does biblical hope look like?

The Bible has much to say about hope. A proper definition of biblical hope is having a complete and total inner peace with confident expectation of an outcome. Romans 8:24-25 says, "For in this hope we were saved. But hope that is seen is no hope at all. Who hopes for what he already has? But if we hope for what we do not yet have, we wait for it patiently." This is the confident outcome that causes us as believers to persevere, waiting for the blessed hope of our salvation.

One of my favorite verses of the Bible deals with hope, too. Jeremiah 29:11-14 says, "'For I know the plans I have for you,' declares the LORD, 'plans to prosper you and not to harm you, plans to give you *hope* and a future. Then you will call upon me and come and pray to me, and I will listen to you. You will seek me and find me when you seek me with all your heart. I will be found by you,' declares the LORD," (emphasis added). Although this verse was written to the nation of Israel during a specific time and for a specific purpose, it still can be applied to our daily lives today. God has a plan for us, and we should never forget that. Verse 11 says, "*plans to give you a hope* and future" (emphasis added). It gives me great comfort and encouragement and brings joy to my heart knowing that the Creator of the universe has plans just for Greg Von Tobel. It teaches that hope is a gift from God when it says, "to give you." God has given me a gift of hope. What an incredible gift!

The second part of that verse says that God is giving us a future. This is another great comfort when we are walking through a soul-shaking crisis. When I am in front of inmates in a prison, I will quote Jeremiah 29:11-12 and say, "Men, isn't that all we really want in life—the promise of hope for a better future?" At that point, many of the inmates begin nodding their heads. Then I tell them, "That blessed hope can only be found in God's Son, Jesus Christ."

I am totally confident that this verse states that God has a plan for each of us. This one verse has sustained me through many trials in my life. I remember the first time I heard another believer quote this verse. I stopped him immediately and asked where the verse could be found in the Bible. I wrote the reference down on my hand, ran home, looked it up, and then meditated on it. I later memorized it and started using it in my sermons to inmates.

Many times, inmates who hear it for the first time react the same way. They write it down! I believe they do this because they realize that a life without hope is a miserable existence. Life without hope loses its resolve and its purpose. The truth is that you can either have hope in your life or not. But remember that as a believer, as long as you have breath in your lungs, you should have hope in your soul. We should all pity the person who feels there is no hope in life.

I suspect having no hope in life is the driving factor behind 100% of suicides—people who have emotional pain so deep in their lives they feel that they can't overcome it. They have lost all hope. The Bible says something to help those who feel that way; Jeremiah says that God has a plan for your life.

These verses in Jeremiah 29:11-12 are verses that every believer should commit to memory, for two good reasons. First, remember them because as we remain on this side of eternity, we will continue to have trials. With true biblical hope, you can prevail during those trials, but without hope, you will shrivel up and die inside living the remainder of your days in despair. Second, remember them so you can offer this hope to those who are walking through tremendous trials themselves. I have known many inmates who have managed to live out abundant lives in prison, even with decades of incarceration ahead of them, because they have clung to these verses.

Do you remember Eeyore from the Winnie-the-Pooh books by A. A. Milne? Eeyore was the glum donkey who found no good in anything. We all know someone who is an Eeyore, those people who are pessimistic, gloomy, and depressed. They have the-sky-is-falling outlook on life. These Eeyore personality types are typically not found in major leadership roles. Eeyores normally don't have a reason to hope. Fortunately, I am an optimist by nature. I don't particularly like hanging out with the Eeyores of life for very long. For the optimists of the world, being around them for too long is draining. Not to say that we dislike them; after all, they are God's children, too. In fact, there have been times when an Eeyore in my life has said something profound that caused me to stop and think about a risk that I had not seriously considered. My point is that if the world was made up only of optimists, the world would be in complete chaos. We need Eeyore's in the world to help us think clearly and preserve peace, even if they sometimes seem hopeless. It is our job as leaders to then teach them that even in their personality they can have hope.

I'll end this chapter with this: Christian leadership must prevail. Hope must prevail. Hope must soar to new heights in good times and must prevail in tough times. Leadership always hopes. What can you do as a leader to display hopefulness for those you lead?

CHAPTER 16
LEADERSHIP ALWAYS PERSEVERES

If you want to be a great leader today, you need to learn to burn your boats. In 1519, Hernán Cortés arrived in the new world with his six hundred men. To ensure that none of them would flee, he ordered the boats be burned. In essence, Cortés was telling the men, they could either prevail or die, but they could not *retreat*. Years later, he succeeded in conquering the Aztec empire.

Cortés knew how to be a powerful leader. He knew that he had to eliminate his men's option for retreat, even if times became rough later. Cortés never gave up on his mission and did not allow his men to do so either. His leadership always persevered.

I am also reminded of Sir Ernest Shackleton, who led the ill-fated expedition to Antarctica on the ship, *Endurance*. History tells us that the *Endurance* was destroyed after it became lodged in a sheet of ice. On October 27, 1915 Shackleton ordered the crew to abandon ship (which was later crushed by the ice) and camp out on the icy terrains. For the next 497 days, the twenty-eight men engaged in a harrowing battle for survival. Through Shackleton's leadership, not one man was lost. Amid crisis, Shackleton had understood that the stakes were—life or death. There had been no third option.

In the end, Shackleton, along with several of his men, sailed 800 miles to South Georgia in a small dingy. It took them sixteen days to arrive at the nearest whaling station.

Once recuperated, it then took several months before he could rescue his remaining crew who were still on Elephant Island. Shackleton never gave up on his men. His men never gave up on him. Leadership should always persevere.

One of my favorite passages of the Bible that illustrates the perseverance of leadership is 2 Samuel 23:9-11. It tells the story of one of David's mighty men, Eleazar. This is the only time this particular Eleazar is mentioned in the Bible.

> Next to him was Eleazar son of Dodai the Ahohite. As one of the three mighty men, he was with David when they taunted the Philistines gathered [at Pas Dammim] for battle. Then the men of Israel retreated, but he stood his ground and struck down the Philistines till his hand grew tired and froze to the sword. The LORD brought about a great victory that day.

What an amazing example of perseverance! Eleazar had been one of David's mighty men who fought in his army against the Philistines. We are not told the reason, but apparently the army retreated, they had left Eleazar out in the field all alone with the enemy army bearing down on him. At that point, Eleazar had to decide whether to retreat with the rest of the army or to stand his ground. It would have been easier for Eleazar to have retreated with his army. Although no one would have faulted him for retreating, he didn't. What do you think was going through his mind when he saw his fellow soldiers running in the opposite direction? I am sure he had moments where he thought of retreating himself.

Eleazar was wired differently than the other soldiers who were retreating. Maybe he was even like Elisha who didn't see with physical eyes but with spiritual eyes. In 2 Kings 6:17 Elisha prayed for his servant to see with spiritual eyes, "Then the LORD opened the servant's eyes, and he looked and saw the hills full of horses and chariots of fire all around Elisha."

The Bible continues in 2 Samuel 23, "But Eleazar stood his ground and struck down the Philistines till his hand grew tired and froze to the sword." Eleazar was a leader who stood his ground and persevered. Verse 10 states, "The LORD brought about a great victory that day."

When faced with insurmountable odds, it is our fleshly nature to flee to the path of least resistance. We should ask ourselves, "Is that what God wants us to do?"

Gideon is another example of someone who did not flee when confronted with insurmountable odds. The Midianites were oppressing Israel, and God chose and prepared Gideon to be the commander of the army. God didn't want the nation to boast about their strategic military power, so he whittled the army down from thirty-two hundred to three hundred. With this army of three hundred fighting men, the Lord led Gideon and his army up against an army of one hundred and thirty-two thousand soldiers. It is our nature to travel the path of least resistance and pain. However, godly leadership always trusts and perseveres. The Apostle Paul is the quintessential example of this:

> Are they servants of Christ? (I am out of my mind to talk like this.) I am more. I have worked much harder, been in prison more frequently, been flogged more severely, and been exposed to death again and again. Five times I received from the Jews the forty lashes minus one. Three times I was beaten with rods, once I was stoned, three times I

was shipwrecked, I spent a night and a day in the open sea, I have been constantly on the move. I have been in danger from rivers, in danger from bandits, in danger from my own countrymen, in danger from Gentiles; in danger in the city, in danger in the country, in danger at sea; and in danger from false brothers. I have labored and toiled and have often gone without sleep; I have known hunger and thirst and have often gone without food; I have been cold and naked. Besides everything else, I face daily the pressure of my concern for all the churches (2 Cor 11:23-28).

In this passage, Paul defends himself against his critics. When I first read this passage as a new believer, I couldn't believe what I was reading. Why would anyone go through *any* of these trials, let alone *all* of them? Paul had steadfastness. Perseverance.

We have a mindset in America that if the work is not being constantly blessed by God, there is something wrong with the ministry or its leader. We pass judgment on them. However, if the Apostle Paul had been under the authority of an American missionary agency, they would have yanked Paul off the mission field and sent him away for reassessment therapy. From the human point of view, one could conclude from this passage that God was *not* blessing Paul. In fact, the opposite is true—God allowed Paul to walk through those trials for us.

If Paul had ever given up, where would we be today? Much of our Christian doctrine, through the divine inspiration of the Holy Spirit, has come through the Apostle Paul. If Paul had given up, we would be without about two-thirds of the New Testament. But he persevered and did not give up. He kept going, even after several floggings. Leadership always perseveres.

I must admit that if I were to go through all that Paul went through, I am not sure I would have the same staying power he had. I would probably give up, and then I would think of myself as a failure. I would ask myself, "What's wrong with me? What's wrong with the vision? What am I doing wrong? Why isn't this being blessed by God?" I am confident I would also have well-meaning family and friends say, "Von Tobel, what are you doing? This is not working. Come home. Your efforts are not being blessed by God." But Paul didn't give up. He kept going, even unto death.

Leadership always perseveres.

Not only did Paul go through many physical hardships, he also went through a good deal of emotional pain when people betrayed and deserted him. If that had been me, I think these betrayals would have been my breaking point.

As leaders, we all have had people who have deserted us in our time of need. But leadership should always persevere. Let us take our cues from the Apostle Paul. May his life story teach us how to stay the course through the trials the Lord allows into our lives. Let us never forget Romans 11:29 which states, "For God's gift and his call are irrevocable." If we are called into ministry, let us never forget that His call on our lives is irrevocable. Never leave your position. Stand firm and run the race marked out for you. Remember, leadership always perseveres.

CHAPTER 17
LEADERSHIP NEVER FAILS

Leadership never fails. Of course, we know this is not a correct statement. Leadership does fail. Many times, in fact, that failure is colossal. To say leadership will never fail is like saying we will never sin. As humans, we do not have the power to stop sinning altogether. However, we *do* have the power to be more Christ-like. While it is not within our power to make correct decisions 100% of the time, as we mature as leaders, our percentage of good decisions should significantly start to outweigh the bad.

Because we often fail, however, leaders must always be on guard with their reputation. Remember that one decision can destroy a reputation forever. You could have spent a lifetime developing a great standing as a leader, only to have that standing evaporate in a heartbeat because of one terrible decision. For the rest of your days, you will only be remembered for that one horrific error in judgement, and not for your accomplishments.

There are so many notable people who are now only remembered for the terrible decisions they made. Among them are: Pete Rose for betting on games in which he played or managed, Tonya Harding for her involvement with the assault on a fellow ice skater, President Bill Clinton for his affair with an intern, President Richard Nixon for the Watergate scandal, and Senator Ted Kennedy for the Chappaquiddick scandal. The Christian community is also not without its own leaders who have damaged their reputations with poor decisions. Examples are Jim and Tammy Bakker, Robert Tilton, Ted Haggard, and Jimmy Swaggart. These people will forever be remembered not for the good they did (or could have done), but for that one mistake (or series of related mistakes) that tarnished them for life. James 1:14-15 says,

> But each one is tempted when by his own evil desire, he is dragged away and enticed. Then, after desire has conceived, it gives birth to sin; and sin, when it is full grown, gives birth to death.

These are incredibly wise and sobering words from James, the half-brother of Jesus. This is the *circle of life* of sin. We are all tempted daily. Temptation is not sin. However, temptation becomes sin when we linger a nanosecond longer on the ungodly thoughts that enter our minds than we should. Sin then grows when we follow through with actions. Therefore, we must train our minds to take every thought captive in obedience to Christ, not allowing any sinful thoughts to master us (2 Cor 10:5).

None of the famous people I mentioned above started out the way they ended. None of them suddenly awoke one morning and said to themselves, "I think I will go out and make some terrible choices today!" Instead, they conceived evil desires in their mind. They nurtured those desires. Eventually, they acted on those desires.

Be on your guard not to make the same mistake. Make sure you have a strong circle of people around you who will hold you accountable for your actions. Do not let one destructive thought turn into destructive actions that will permanently destroy your reputation.

I am reminded of King David, a man after God's own heart. I love David and the stories in the Bible about his life. He is, among many others on my list, someone that I plan to track down and meet when I get to Heaven. However, even though David did many good things in his life, he is also known for his affair with Bathsheba and the subsequent murder of her husband, Uriah.

The same goes for King Solomon. Even though he did much good during his reign, he is also remembered for his hundreds of foreign wives and concubines.

How can we protect ourselves from making that one fatal mistake, or even a series of related mistakes? Let me give you what I call the *iron dome protectors*. Let's start with the example of the Billy Graham Modesto Manifesto. Named after the small town in California where this manifesto was created, the Modesto Manifesto was a set of biblical behavioral standards that Billy Graham and his team built together, right there in a motel room. Their evangelical pastor had called on his leaders to create the manifesto in 1948, a time when it was especially important to mitigate exposure to sex, money, and power scandals.[6]

In 1948, Billy Graham, Cliff Barrows, George Beverly Shea, and Grady Wilson crafted these first four points called the Modesto Manifesto:[7]

1. **The first point** on our combined list was money. Nearly all evangelists at that time—including us—were supported by love offerings taken at the meetings. The temptation to wring as much money as possible out of an audience, often with strong emotional appeals, was too great for some evangelists. In addition, there was

---

[6] Quora, "What is the Modesto Manifesto," Quora, accessed February 22, 2018, https://www.quora.com/What-is-the-Modesto-Manifesto.
[7] Quora, "On This Date: The Modesto Manifesto - The Billy Graham Library Blog," The Billy Graham Library, accessed October 26, 2017, https://billygrahamlibrary.org/on-this-date-the-modesto-manifesto.

little or no accountability for finances. It was a system that was easy to abuse—and led to the charge that evangelists were in it only for the money.

2. **The second item** on the list was the danger of sexual immorality. We all knew of evangelists who had fallen into immorality while separated from their families by travel. We pledged among ourselves to avoid any situation that would have even the appearance of compromise or suspicion. From that day on, I did not travel, meet or eat alone with a woman other than my wife. We determined that the Apostle Paul's mandate to the young pastor Timothy would be ours as well: "Flee ... youthful lusts" (2 Tim 1:22, KJV).

3. **Our third concern** was the tendency of many evangelists to carry on their work apart from the local church, even to criticize local pastors and churches openly and scathingly. We were convinced, however, that this was not only counterproductive but also wrong from the Bible's standpoint. We determined to cooperate with all who would cooperate with us in the public proclamation of the Gospel, and to avoid an antichurch or anti-clergy attitude.

4. **The fourth and final issue** was publicity. The tendency among some evangelists was to exaggerate their successes or to claim higher attendance numbers than they really had. This likewise discredited evangelism and brought the whole enterprise under suspicion. It often made the press so suspicious of evangelists that they refused to take notice of their work. In Modesto we committed ourselves to integrity in our publicity and our reporting.

The four points above are the "Gold Standard" for any church, parachurch organization, or Christian leader. They are priceless. They are timeless. In the seventy-two years since the Modesto Manifesto was created, society has changed immensely. If I may take editorial liberty, let me add other points that I believe should be included in the *iron dome of protectors*.

1. **Don't make decisions based on fear:** One of the worst things an organization can do is to chart a course based on fear—fear of lawsuits, fear of losing tithes, fear of staff leaving, fear of the unknown, or the fear of fabricated scenarios. Making decisions from a place of fear takes God out of the equation. Decisions based on fear will cause suspicion between you and those you serve. I have sat in many meetings where attorneys were present. Attorneys, due to the nature of their industry, are responsible for pointing out all the possible outcomes of a situation. Some attorneys even create doomsday scenarios for their clients. I am not saying that you should not have counsel as needed, but guard your heart when seeking direction from the Lord.

2. **Transparency:** The three most important things in real estate are location, location, location. The three most important things in ministry are transparency, transparency, transparency. Be transparent with your constituency. If you make a mistake, be transparent about it. Own up to it. Most people are very forgiving. Hiding information leads to hiding more information. Nothing will cause more pain in a crisis than a leader who is *perceived* as concealing the truth.

3. **Be Open Handed:** Hold things loosely in your hands. This includes goals, dreams, policies, procedures, and ministry and financial resources. Luke 12:48 states, "From everyone who has been given much, much will be demanded." That doesn't mean you are a doormat for the world, giving everything away such as copyrights or intellectual rights. It does mean having policies in place for when someone needs your help. Give as the Lord provides and how He leads. Hotels have concierges and hospitality coordinators to be available for their clients in their times of need. People who staff these positions are typically the more outgoing and friendly personality types. They are individuals who have the gift of helps. All churches and non-profits should make use of those with these same gifts—those who are genuinely interested in helping others in need.

We will never be perfect in our leadership abilities or in the daily decisions we make. Good decisions, of course, will help us grow in our leadership, adding to our credibility as good leaders. As counterintuitive as it sounds, bad decisions will also cause growth as well. Failure has the capability of leading to significant *exponential* growth because of the pain it causes. If you are a normal person, you will never want to experience that pain ever again in your life. If the mistake is painful enough, not only will you do everything in your power not to repeat it, but you will show others how to avoid the mistake you made. Most mistakes are forgivable and will not do permanent damage to you or your organization. But be on guard against those that can do both.

Acting Secretary of the Navy Thomas B. Modly was recently fired for his disparaging remarks he made publicly.

These remarks were directed at Captain Brett Crozier, Captain of the Aircraft Carrier USS *Theodore Roosevelt* regarding the outbreak of the COVID-19 virus on his ship. The first time I heard the sound bite, I knew that he would lose his job. And he soon did. It was a poor leadership decision on Modly's part to speak out the way he did and in the tone of voice he did against Captain Crozier.

Similarly, actor Jussie Smollet also concocted a story that two of President Trump's supporters yelled homophobic slurs at him and assaulted him. The truth soon came out that this was not the case, however, and Jussie was fired from the TV role he had.

Another famous poor decision by a public figure was when former President Clinton had a sexual tryst with an intern. The truth eventually came out. This was a poor decision made by one of the most powerful men in the world. These are the kinds of decisions that can permanently tarnish reputations and potentially destroy careers.

Absent decisions of the magnitude of the examples above, you will survive the inevitable bad choice you make. I find that most of my leadership growth actually comes from when I have made bad decisions, rather than good ones. I find exponential leadership growth comes from those bad decisions. Never be afraid to fail. Instead, be afraid of when you fail and don't learn from your mistakes.

Someone once said, "We are all standing in the middle of the railroad tracks. We are either moving forward or we are standing still. If we are standing still, it is only a matter of time until we are run over." Thus, we need to excel in our strengths.

Gregory E. Von Tobel

"Since you are eager to have spiritual gifts, try to excel in gifts that build up the church."

Apostle Paul

1 Corinthians 14:12

UNIT 3
EXECUTION

Love is patient, love is kind.
It does not envy, it does not boast,
it is not proud.
It is not rude, it is not self-seeking,
it is not easily angered, it keeps no record of
wrongs.
Love does not delight in evil but rejoices with
truth.
It always protects, always trust,
always hopes, always perseveres.
Love never fails.

Apostle Paul

1 Corinthians 13:4-8

CHAPTER 18
SELF-EVALUATION

You have now been through fourteen leadership principles that, if implemented correctly, will launch you to your next level of leadership. You may find that while you have already rocked some of these principles, there are still some you have miserably failed to practice. I know this because I have done the same. This is okay, because—as we discussed earlier—we often learn more from our failures than our successes. The important thing is to make sure you do learn from those failures.

The world needs new leaders. The world needs Christian leaders. The Christian community needs godly leaders to help steer the ship in these turbulent times. Even before the COVID-19 crisis hit, I thought the wheels of the world were flying off in all directions. In Chapter 1 of this book, I reprinted an excerpt from my first book, *Staving off Disaster: A Journey in Spiritual Fasting*, listing out some of the maladies I saw occurring in our world in 2016. Not much has changed since then.

Not only does the world need solid Christian leaders, but we need new, millennial-age leaders, too. These younger brothers and sisters are the next generation to lead and we desperately need them to be firmly grounded in the faith and in biblical leadership principles. We need the younger generation of soon-to-be Christian leaders to sharpen their leadership swords and wield them with biblical authority. I pen these words praying there will be hundreds if not thousands of millennial readers who will take to heart what has been written about leadership principles in this book. We need millennial leaders with their swords in the air contending for the faith.

In 2011 John Maxwell created the five levels of leadership positions. Maxwell has written many books on leadership, which I have devoured, but these five principles have been a major influence in growing me as a leader. These five leadership levels are brilliant. I have summarized his levels based on his website and emphasized quotes which stand out to me.[8]

Level 1 – Position

This is the entry point of leadership. It happens when a person is simply appointed to a leadership role. Maxwell says it, "*requires no ability or effort to achieve*." While this may be true in many cases, I would hope that those making the appointment would see the potential of a person before making a blind appointment. However, that is not his point. His point is that a newly appointed "leader" can't rely only on his or her position to get subordinates to follow. They will follow only because they desire to continue to be paid. They follow because they feel they have no choice.

People who rely on their position as a leader and don't mature to higher levels will have problems. Maxwell points out that they "may find it *difficult to work with volunteers*." You can see this because their only influence is a result of their subordinates' belief that they have no choice.

---

[8] John Maxwell, "The 5 Levels of Leadership," John Maxwell, August 30, 2016, https://www.johnmaxwell.com/blog/the-5-levels-of-leadership1.

Volunteers don't have to follow because they don't need the job.

Level 2 – Permission

As you develop in your leadership, Maxwell says the next level "is based on ***relationship***." To advance to this level you must genuinely like the people who are working for you. This is done by getting to know your people. You treat them with respect and let them know that they have value. This fosters a relationship of trust and respect within a positive environment. This applies to more than just a work environment, but also applies to your home, recreational activities, social groups, and church. Maxwell calls this level "permission" because the people who are subordinate to you "choose to follow because they want to." They have given you permission to lead. If you apply the love principles found in Unit 2 based on 1 Corinthians 13:4-8, you will develop into a level 2 leader in every aspect of your life.

Level 3 – Production

Maxwell labels this level as "production" because leaders at this level have learned how to do more than have a relationship with their people. They have learned to motivate them. When their people are properly motivated, they "GTD – ***get things done***!" As this leader's team is getting things done, they get positive "***results***." It is an interesting phenomenon that getting results builds credibility and influence with peers and higher management. People are following not just because of their relationship but because of the leader's track record of getting things done.

This level builds on itself. When work is getting done, everyone benefits. Morale is up, profits are up, and people don't quit out of frustration. This is the level where leaders can become a change agent. With this kind of team and the efficiency they bring, you will be able to take on harder problems and more complex projects.

At this point, Maxwell notes that "Leading and influencing others becomes fun." However, he cautions that as one advances to each new level, you still must keep doing everything you do in the lower levels. They build on each other.

Level 4 – People Development

Maxwell says this level "can be summed up in one word: **reproduction**." Maxwell must have understood this based on the way Jesus developed His disciples. Jesus invested in His disciples and helped them grow. When He left, His instruction was to do the same by going and making disciples of all nations (Matt 28:19). At this level you must do the same thing.

At this point, you are no longer looking out only for your own interests or even your team's. You are looking out for your entire organization. Your organization needs more leaders to accomplish its mission. The best way to get them is to develop them. Whether you start with "rough fishermen" or "cunning tax collectors," you will want to reproduce people who will do the same as you are doing.

Maxwell says, "***The more you raise up new leaders, the more you will change the lives of all members of the team***." As you develop people, your leadership grows because you have made significant investments in their lives. You have become a mentor, and this often leads to a relationship that is "***likely to last a lifetime***." This doesn't happen by chance. You need to be intentional and make it a priority in your life if you want to become a leader as described in the next level.

Level 5 – Pinnacle

This level of leadership is at the top, or I should say over the top, which is why Maxwell labels it the "pinnacle." Not many people achieve this level because it is the most challenging. As mentioned in the previous level, it requires intentionality. It requires the perseverance of a lifetime. That means persevering in developing yourself and others as described in the previous levels. When you have this kind of perseverance, other take notice and your "leadership gains a positive **reputation**."

Maxwell points out that the payoff to achieving this level is great. The payoff is seen in the organization as well as the legacy for that they do. "People follow them because of who they are and what they represent." They lead well beyond their position, organization, or industry.

I must comment that there is danger for anyone who achieves or desires to achieve this level. The first is that it requires perseverance. Perseverance comes from hard work. Romans 5:3-4 puts it this way, "We know that suffering produces perseverance; perseverance, character; and character, hope." I believe that without character in addition to perseverance, you will not have any hope of advancing to level 5. The second warning is that achieving this level can be a significant temptation towards pride. We must always remember that the Lord is the one who exalts or brings down (Dan 2:21). We must take heed of Peter's admonition, "All of you, clothe yourselves with humility toward one another, because, 'God opposes the proud but gives grace to the humble.' Humble yourselves, therefore, under God's mighty hand, that he may lift you up in due time" (1 Peter 5:5-6). If you achieve this level, it is because God has enabled and guided you into it. So give Him the credit and, "whatever you do, do it all for the glory of the God" (1 Cor 10:31).

These five levels of leadership, by Maxwell, are very useful for self-evaluation and motivation. It doesn't matter if you are a Level 1 leader or even a Level 5 leader, there is always room for improvement. It takes a lifetime to become a Level 5 leader. Level 5 leaders have national platforms like Billy Graham, Franklin Graham, Luis Palau, Sir Winston Churchill, George Washington, Abraham Lincoln, and Queen Elizabeth. Most of us will never attain that level of leadership.

This concludes *Biblical Leadership in Turbulent Times – Part One.* This book lays the foundation for the three-part series by giving you an understanding of the core values for Christian leadership. Part Two will focus on physical attributes of Christian leaders. Before you move to *Biblical Leadership in Turbulent Times – Part Two,* complete the exercises in Exhibit B to determine your current level of leadership. This exercise will assist you in determining which areas you need to polish.

APPENDIX

EXHIBIT A
THE POWER OF THREE

Because prison ministry mission trips are like no other (in terms of the miles traveled, work hours in the day, and bumpy roads), it is truly important for all members of the team to learn the power of three. During these trips, emotions are high, energy is down, accommodations are less than expected; furthermore, creature comforts are nowhere to be found at these times. Before you know it, you and your team are embroiled in backbiting, hurt feelings, and a lot of sulking. This is certainly not honoring to the Lord or edifying to the Body. Inevitably, someone will come back from a trip saying, "I will never go on another trip if John Doe is going too!"

If you haven't yet experienced a situation similar to this, wait, you likely will. However, I believe they can be avoided. I believe these kinds of issues are a result of inadequate training. If your team is well trained, these problems can be headed off before you leave America. As believers and leaders in Christ, we are called to a higher standard than the world's.

The power of three can be found in five sentences with only three words.

1. **<u>Love one another:</u>** This seems simple enough but it isn't, especially when you are tired, hungry, hot and uncomfortable. However, Jesus said it, and therefore, we should endeavor to live it out in our lives.

111

2. **Zip your lips:** I am often amazed at things that fall out of people's mouths. "Zip your lips" means exactly what it says—ZIP YOUR LIPS! The book of James talks about what great fires can be set off by the tongue. As a humorous word picture, try to imagine everyone on your team with great big zippers for lips.

3. **Die to self:** Often, the principles of loving one another and zipping your lips are not enough to head off a firestorm. You must then move to the next level of biblical principles, die to self. Self is a powerful enemy to God-ordained goals. Puffed up self is pride, which keeps us from the next step.

4. **Keep short accounts:** The Bible teaches us that perfect love keeps no records of wrongs. People on mission trips often keep records of others' perceived offenses. This is not good! This causes people to be preoccupied taking their eyes and focus off of Jesus and the mission.

5. **Build others up:** This can happen in several ways:

   - **Verbally** – Giving someone compliments in private or in public.
   - **Written form** – Writing an encouraging note can go a long way towards encouraging someone on a trip.
   - **Servant leader** – Doing something for someone when it is not expected.
   - **Mentally** – This is the hard one, but if you can find something good in someone, you will then be able to overcome any offenses that Satan will throw your way.

The power of three! We must endeavor to live out the power of three in our own lives as well as teach new teammates to do the same.

EXHIBIT B
SELF-REFLECTION TEST

Take a moment to complete this self-examination test. You will need your spouse to help you out. On the left side of each number, rate yourself in each of the respective categories by assigning a value between one and ten, ten being the highest, one being the lowest. Be honest. Once you complete your self-evaluation, fold the paper over so your spouse can't see how you rated yourself. Have him or her rate you, too on the right side.

Does your spouse see you the same way as you see yourself? If no, then it would be good to discuss that with him or her. If you really want to obtain a good snapshot of yourself and your leadership, you could also give this to one of your peers at work. Give your spouse and co-worker confidence that there will be no collateral damage based on how they rate you. None! Also, understand a co-worker will not have the ability to rate you in all of the categories as well as your spouse will.

1. I am patient with my family
2. I am patient with my co-workers
3. I am patient with strangers
4. I am kind to people I know
5. I am kind to strangers
6. I don't think envious thoughts
7. I am not proud or arrogant
8. I am not rude to my family
9. I am not rude to strangers
10. I am not self-seeking

11. I am not easily outwardly angered
12. I am not easily inwardly angered
13. I keep no record of wrongs
14. I don't delight in evil
15. I always attempt to protect my family, friends, and staff
16. I always trust in people to do the right thing
17. I always trust employees as having the right motives
18. I always hope for positive outcomes
19. I always persevere through projects as well as trials
20. I seldom fail in my leadership abilities

Instructions:

1. Do not read these instructions until you have taken the self-evaluation test.
2. Add up your score on the left side. If you have a total combined score of between 140-200 points, you are doing well. However, there is always room for improvement.
3. If you have a combined score less than 140 points, your leadership reputation could be in jeopardy.
4. If you rated yourself as less than 7 on any attribute, you need to take immediate action to correct the problem.
5. If you rated yourself as less than 5 on any attribute, you need immediate help in changing course.
6. The same goes for your spouse's ratings. If he or she rates you as less than 5 on any attribute, you should take immediate, corrective action.

If your spouse rates you two or more points lower than how you rated yourself on an attribute, you have a perception problem.

EXHIBIT C
CORRECTIVE ACTION

1. Using the list in Exhibit B, list all attributes that you rated yourself less than 7.
2. Write out a problem statement for each. What do you see are the symptoms of the problem? What pain do you experience from this problem? What needs to change for this problem to be corrected?
3. List three possible action items you can take to correct this weakness.

Attribute number and name:

Problem Statement: Allow the Holy Spirit to reveal you why you are weak in this area. List this in the form of a problem statement.

Corrective action: What three things can you do to correct this leadership deficiency?

1.

2.

3.

ABOUT PRISONERS FOR CHRIST OUTREACH MINISTRIES

Let me take a few more minutes of your time and tell you a little more about Prisoners For Christ Outreach Ministries (PFC). PFC is a ministry dedicated to taking the Gospel of Jesus Christ to the institutions of the world. As of the close of 2019, we had over 1,500 volunteers worldwide and we are growing every day. Last year, our volunteers conducted an average of 510 church services per month, more than 16 services per day. PFC had a yearly attendance count of over 967,000 at our services last year, with over 66,700 men, women, and children accepting Jesus Christ as Lord and Savior for the first time.

Originally started in the state of Washington, PFC has field offices in eighteen different countries, including Burkina Faso, Burundi, Cameroon, Congo-DRC, Ethiopia, India, Kenya, Malawi, Nepal, Niger, Nigeria, Russia, Rwanda, Sierra Leonne, Tanzania, the Philippines, Togo, and Uganda, with more than ten other countries waiting to be accepted.

In addition, PFC has a two-year Bible study correspondence course and a pen-pal program, as well as our national inmate newspaper, *Yard Out*, for inmates here in the United States. We exist for the sole purpose of sharing the love of Christ to the lost in the prisons of the world.

Our major objective is to win souls to Christ. Our secondary objective is to equip the saints to do good works while in the sphere of prison ministry. Whether you are an

117

individual prison volunteer going into one institution, or whether you are a part of a larger team, or even perhaps a volunteer in your church's prison outreach, we are interested in you! We are interested in your development as a minister of the Gospel. So please avail yourself of our training and the printed resources found on our web page, www.prisonersforchrist.org.

If the Lord should ever tug on your heart to be a part of the PFC team worldwide, we have several opportunities of involvement for you.

1. If you have a loved one in prison and desire some Christian literature be sent to that person, please go online at www.prisonersforchrist.org to submit a literature request.

2. If you would like to receive our current annual report or register for our newsletter, either in print or electronically, please go to the website to request copies.

3. If you would like to volunteer or develop a PFC outpost in your state, please go to the website and ask for our franchise brochure. See more on the franchise ministry in the subsequent pages.

4. If you were blessed by this book, you can donate either by mailing a check to our PFC offices or by giving online through our web page. Please go to the same site and at the bottom of the page and click "Give."

Whether you are here in the United States or living in another part of the world, please consider joining the family of PFC. However, if you are a part of another existing prison ministry, stay where you are and be the best prison ministry volunteer for that organization. In other words, "Bloom where you are planted!"

Feel free to connect with us in one of several ways:

1. Mailing address: Prisoners For Christ (PFC), PO Box 1530, Woodinville, WA 98072
2. Web page: www.prisonersforchrist.org
3. PFC Facebook: https://www.facebook.com/Prisoners-for-Christ-Outreach-Ministries-76125072756
4. Office phone: (425) 483-4151
5. Personal Facebook: https://www.facebook.com/gregvontobel

BIBLIOGRAPHY

Books

Scott, Stuart. *From Pride to Humility: A Biblical Perspective*. Bemidji, MN: Focus Pub., 2002.

Web

Bible Study Tools, s.v., "hope." Accessed May 16, 2020. https://www.biblestudytools.com/ dictionary/hope.

Goalcast. "Martin Luther King Jr.: The Most Important Time of Your Life." Goalcast. Accessed February 28, 2017. https://www.goalcast.com/2017/02/28/the-most-important-time-of-your-life-martin-luther-king-jr.

GotQuestions.org. "Home." GotQuestions.org. Accessed November 14, 2012. https://www.gotquestions.org/love-not-delight-evil-rejoices-truth.html.

John Maxwell. "The 5 Levels of Leadership." John Maxwell. Accessed August 30, 2016. https://www.johnmaxwell.com/blog/the-5-levels-of-leadership1.

Merriam Webster, s.v. "hope." Accessed May 16, 2020. https://www.merriam-webster.com/dictionary/hope.

Quora. "What is the Modesto Manifesto." Quora. Accessed February 22, 2018. https://www.quora.com/What-is-the-Modesto-Manifesto.

Quora. "On This Date: The Modesto Manifesto - The Billy Graham Library Blog." The Billy Graham Library. Accessed October 26, 2017. https://billygrahamlibrary.org/on-this-date-the-modesto-manifesto.

Trent Hamm. "Lincoln's Axe and Frugality." The Simple Dollar. Accessed May 15, 2020. https://www.thesimpledollar.com/financial-wellness/lincolns-axe-and-frugality.

OTHER RESOURCES

Got Problems?

I know you do. Kids are going sideways. Accidents happen. Relationships are strained. Houses are being foreclosed upon. Jobs are being lost. Brain tumors are being discovered. Car engines are blowing up. Identities are being stolen. Pornography can be accessed on smartphones. Hackers are hacking. Kids are overdosing. College women are being date-raped. Planes are going down. ISIS is on the move. New viruses are being discovered. Home invasions are happening. Children are bearing children. Fathers are leaving their posts. Kids are killing kids in schools. Christians are being martyred and imprisoned around the world for their faith. Sharia law is coming to the United States. The problems go on and on and on. It seems as if the wheels are coming off the world, and they are.

- Do you have a crisis in your life?
- Do you have a friend or family member walking through the fires of life right now?
- How are you going to survive in this world where the wheels are coming off?
- What are the mountains in your life needing to be blown away?
- How are you going to protect your family in a world which is self-destructing before your very eyes?

Christian believer, if you or someone you know is going through the fires of trials and tribulations, this book on biblical fasting is for you. Biblical fasting is a powerful spiritual tool virtually ignored by the body of Christ today. Author Greg Von Tobel explains the correct motives for fasting, the wrong ways to fast, the biblical precedence for the church today to fast, and outlines ten steps to kick-starting your lifelong fasting discipline.

Prison Ministry Training

Part 1—Getting Started in Prison Ministry

Modern-day prison ministry can feel like an uncertain and daunting path to navigate alone. Even for those who feel the calling, it can be a challenge to understand how best to begin.

Now you can learn time-tested and proven methods from one of the world's most renowned experts in prison ministry. An unrivaled training guide, *Prison Ministry Training, Basic Training Part 1: Getting Started in Prison Ministry* is composed of multiple sections for the reader. Once you've completed it, you will have an understanding of the following.

- Why one might pursue prison ministry
- The biblical reasons for participating in prison ministry
- How prison ministry changes lives—for the inmate as well as the volunteer
- The enormity of the prison ministry mission field
- The five steps in starting on your own journey in prison ministry
- The six steps in growing a prison ministry
- The four divisions of prison ministry
- An appendix providing valuable insight into the differences in ministry between jails and prisons

Unlike any other book on prison ministry, *Prison Ministry Training* is a completely innovative and contemporary approach to this ministry. With the tools learned, you will have the power to help individuals transform into someone with newfound purpose in God's Kingdom.

Prison Ministry Training

Part 2—Volunteer Recruiting, Training, and Oversight

"You are worrying over things you ought not to worry about. You need to do as Moses did."

"What's that, Rico?"

"The Moses approach, Papa, the Moses approach."

For the author, Gregory E. Von Tobel, this enigmatic advice changed the face of prison ministry for life. Received during the stressful minutes before an important presentation, the gentle reprimand reminded Von Tobel of Moses in Exodus 18. In this passage, Moses, overwhelmed from trying to "do it all" by himself, learns the wisdom of delegation.

Now you can learn time-tested and proven methods from one of the world's most renowned experts in prison ministry. An unrivaled training guide, *Prison Ministry Training, Part 2* is composed of multiple sections for the reader. Once you've completed it, you will have an understanding of the following.

- The hot-potato approach to expanding a prison ministry
- How and where to recruit new volunteers
- How to recruit the younger generation—Millennials and Gen Z
- The code of conduct for volunteers
- The code of conduct for group leaders
- Techniques in overcoming volunteer problems
- A robust appendix with recruiting tools and volunteer applications

Prison Ministry Training

Part 3—Conducting An Effective Bible Study, Church Service, Altar Call, Prison Ministry Network, and Working with Staff

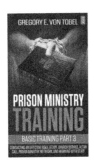

For those who are called to preach the Gospel of Jesus Christ in the jails and prisons, there isn't a great deal of instructive material available. Gregory E. Von Tobel has filled that void. In this third installment of *Prison Ministry Training*, he provides a step-by-step guide for pastors and lay leaders who are inspired to work with offenders. Von Tobel brings over three decades of experience to this concise yet detailed book.

He sketches out exactly how to conduct an effective church service in prison. For the crucial part of the service, the altar call, he maps out the best way to clearly and concisely present the Gospel. Once complete, you will have an understanding of:

- The seven steps to conducting an effective church service
- Preaching tips for the jail setting versus the prison setting
- The importance of doing an altar call
- The six different steps to giving an effective altar call
- The three distinctive styles of delivering an altar call
- Developing a state-wide prison ministry network
- The best ways of working with staff of the prison

ABOUT THE AUTHOR

As a former stockbroker, Gregory E. Von Tobel has been involved in full-time prison missionary work for over thirty years. He is the founder and president of Prisoners For Christ Outreach Ministries (PFC), a ministry dedicated to taking the Gospel of Jesus Christ into the jails, prisons, and juvenile institutions not only in Washington State but also worldwide. PFC has field offices in eighteen foreign countries, including Burkina Faso, Burundi, Cameroon, Congo- DRC, Ethiopia, India, Kenya, Malawi, Nepal, Niger, Nigeria, Russia, Rwanda, Sierra Leonne, Tanzania, The Philippines, Togo, and Uganda.

PFC's volunteers worldwide conduct more than five hundred and ten church services and Bible studies per month, more than sixteen services per day. PFC's national Bible Study Correspondence School has over twenty-five hundred inmates on its student-body roster. Also, PFC's national inmate newspaper, *Yard Out*, is sent to over twelve hundred prison institutions nationally. In addition, PFC has over fifteen hundred volunteers in the ministry worldwide in some capacity, coming from over one-hundred different churches.

Mr. Von Tobel was a stockbroker for eleven years, from 1978 through 1989, for various firms, including EF Hutton & Co. and Shearson Lehman Brothers, when God called him into full-time prison ministry work. On May 14, 1990, God closed one chapter of his life, and on the following day, May 15, 1990, God opened up a whole new chapter. As of 1984, Greg has been ministering in Washington State jails and prisons, six years on a volunteer basis, and the last thirty years as a full-time missionary to those incarcerated.

Mr. Von Tobel has also served on the Governor's Panel of the Department of Corrections' Religious Services Advisory Council, assisting the department in setting religious policies and practices for inmates. In addition, he has served as past president of the Washington Chaplains Association and was a former Duvall City Councilman.

Greg has been married to Rhonda for the past forty-two years. They have three children and five grandchildren.

Made in the USA
Monee, IL
16 September 2022

14125566R00075